1

"Jane Beach has done it again! In her new book, *Freedom... free to be me,* she offers a daily delicious dollop of inspiration and motivation. There is great power to be found in a daily mindfulness practice that brings one's soul and body into alignment in the present moment; read this book *every day* because it will do just that . . . and, in the process, you'll understand how blessed your life already is."

—**Dennis Merritt Jones,** award-winning author of
The Art of Uncertainty: How to Live in the Mystery of Life and Love It,
and *Your (re)Defining Moments: Becoming Who You Were Born to Be*

"I love my morning reading over coffee. I always look for a powerful pick-me-up that starts my day off right. Jane Beach's *Freedom... free to be me* is just the ticket. Short, punchy, and always insightful, every day provides a kernel to ruminate on, a nugget to tease apart, and the seed of an intention to follow. It's the perfect morning companion to set your day up to 'Be the Me' *you* want to be. Enjoy the *Freedom* Jane invites you into and the positive life she helps you envision.

—**Petra Weldes, D.D.,** Spiritual Director, Center for
Spiritual Living, Dallas; co-author of the series *Joyous Freedom Journal, Joyous Living Journal* and *Joyous Abundance Journal*

"Nature flourishes above ground because of a high-quality root system. Likewise, human beings flourish outwardly when establishing a deep rooted inner awareness. The most assured way for us to 'grow our roots' is through devoted practice. Jane Beach continues to be one of the best inner root growing catalysts today, offering up daily guides that open the reader's heart and mind to greater possibility. *Freedom... free to be me* delivers beautifully written devotionals that help us uncover our inherent worth and brilliance.

—**David Ault,** author of *The Grass Is Greener Right Here*

"In her years as minister and mentor to thousands of spiritual seekers, Reverend Jane Beach has consistently and persistently brought people back to a basic mystical teaching: God wants us to be happy. Joy, along with its first cousin's prosperity and health, is a basic birthright of all humanity. Jane Beach activates these truths within us with a short, direct paragraph of wisdom for each day of the year along with a powerful affirmation we can hold in our heart. Joy is who we are, accept it!"

—REV. PATRICK SORAN, Spiritual Director, Center for
Spiritual Living, Denver; Editor, *Creative Thought* magazine;
Contributor, *Science of Mind* magazine.

"Jane Beach's new book *Freedom... free to be me* opens the door to enormous possibility. Transformation awaits, if you're willing to take the next step.

"Life can be messy. Dire circumstances crop up every day. A typical day may be filled with worry, fear and doubt, upset and anger. Stress debilitates not only you but the people around you. But what if those dire circumstances didn't dictate your reactions? What if you didn't feel overwhelmed or stressed out or upset? What if you could choose how you react?

"*Freedom* presents daily reminders about how to view your situation from a different perspective. Complete with simple yet profound tips, this book offers you new choices to help you discover *you*. Not the you filled with negative thoughts, but the you that's energetic, happy, and vibrant. By connecting with your inner wisdom, you *choose* how you want to be, and the universe resonates with you, bringing you more abundance, more happiness, more love. As Beach states so poetically, 'Listen to that silent voice of truth and say yes. Your life of freedom awaits. Follow the pages of *Freedom* and watch a life of magic unfold.'"

—NANETTE LITTLESTONE, *Words of Passion*;
Editor-in-Chief of the *Conscious Life Journal*

"I am so grateful for Jane Beach. She is an artist. One of her fabulous paintings graces the cover of this book. However, Jane's greatest craft is communicating great wisdom with the purity of simplicity. These daily passages are her heart speaking directly to mine. Her messages and the accompanying affirmations are relevant to everyday life and give a sense of community. We are all connected. They also offer an opportunity for a near effortless daily spiritual practice. This book and Jane's heart are welcome additions to my personal daily practice and I recommend it to every student of Life and of self.

—**MARY LAQUET,** United Kingdom

Freedom...
free to be me

Also by Jane Beach

Choices: Choosing me is OK

Remembering Who I Am: A Spiritual Guide to Happiness

3-Part Workbook Series :

How to Build a Relationship with the God of your Understanding:
Part One: Start Where You Are

How to Build a Relationship with the God of your Understanding:
Part Two: Stepping Into Change

How to Build a Relationship with the God of your Understanding:
Part Three: Living Life Fully

Freedom...
free to be me

Daily Reflections and Devotions

JANE BEACH

KENOS PRESS

An Imprint of Six Degrees Publishing Group

Freedom... free to be me
Copyright © 2017 Jane Beach

KENOS PRESS
an Imprint of Six Degrees Publishing Group
5331 S.W. Macadam Avenue, Suite 258
Portland, Oregon 97239

ISBN: 978-1-942497-35-6
eBook ISBN: 978-1-942497-36-3

US Library of Congress Control Number:
2017956166

Published in the United States of America
First Paperback Edition 2017
Kenos Press

Cover Art: Jane Beach © 2017 Jane Beach

Epigraph: Mary Oliver, *No Voyage and Other Poems*,
The Journey

Editorial and Design Supervision: Denise C. Williams

Inquiries: Publisher@SixDegreesPublishing.com

Printed simultaneously in the United States of America,
the United Kingdom and Australia

1 3 5 7 9 10 8 6 4 2

There was a new voice
which you slowly
recognized as your own,
that kept you company
as you strode deeper and deeper
into the world . . .

—MARY OLIVER
(The Journey)

Contents

Foreword

I HAVE BEEN RICHLY BLESSED MANY TIMES OVER in my life. One such time was in August of 2010 when I was in the audience as Jane Beach spoke about her personal discovery that God is real. I was moved at depth and in awe of the way Jane articulated perfectly a gamut of feelings and experiences I'd had, but had never been able to meaningfully express.

Jane crossed my path in the perfect way, at the perfect time. Her passion, openness and honesty touched my heart and I continue to be inspired by her words on a daily basis.

It is no accident this book has found you. Now is the perfect time for *you* to be blessed by the wisdom, compassion, and love of Jane Beach. Let your heart and mind be open to a totally new experience, whether you are already familiar with Jane's work or not.

As your journey into the reflections and devotions inscribed on these pages begins, I invite you to be curious about the answer to this question: Who *is* the 'me' I'm free to be?

How often have you sat in contemplation or personal inquiry about who you really are? I remember being told as a child, "Just who do you think you are young lady?" It wasn't a good thing to hear, as it typically preceded a telling-off. Yet as an adult, and a student of Truth, I find it an all together more inspiring question to sit with. Who am I?

Growing up, I had no role model for the concept that I'm free to be me. I learned from a very young age that I must conform in order to be accepted and acceptable. I received love if I was a 'good girl', if I followed the house rules, if I achieved results and worked hard. This contributed to an overwhelming need to fit in and to squash my true self. What were you raised to believe about having the freedom to be yourself? Most likely it was something very similar to me. Here's the important thing about these beliefs: they are not true!

Each one of us is a perfect expression of Life. We are all equally valuable, unique, worthy, enough (in every way), and deserving (of all Life's abundance). And as you read these passages and allow them to filter into your consciousness, you will discover new ways to think about yourself and your life.

Whether you use this book as a daily guide for inspiration, or a divination tool for your growth, you will be greatly changed if you can be willing to bathe in Jane's words. Simply reading the text will definitely impact you. But, what if you invite each syllable to soak into your very being? What if you take each daily text and seek to embody it in everything you think, say, and do? Embodying these words will slowly, steadily, and permanently change you. This change will enable you to truly embrace personal freedom.

Recognizing the amazing potential for personal transformation within these pages, I think it is even more valuable to seek some clarity about who we are today so that we can be more clear about who we are becoming.

If the words within these pages have the ability to change you at depth (which they do), who is the new you that you are free to be?

Who do you wish to become?

There is, within you, a place that has never been hurt or wounded, never been abandoned or rejected, never felt stupid or hopeless. I humbly suggest that the true, authentic you is desperate to elevate itself beyond the learned helplessness, the frustrations, the shoulds and the shame.

Jane Beach is a master teacher, in every way. Her beautiful book invites you to set yourself free; to remember who you really are, and to embrace and embody that version of yourself fully. You're not here by accident, breathe deeply and take the plunge. Drench yourself in the wisdom within and declare for yourself, "I'm free to be me."

—Juliet Vorster, Author of *Igniting Success Beyond Beliefs:*
How to get from where you are to your greatest yet to be

Introduction

YOU WERE BORN TO LIVE A LIFE THAT'S HAPPY, vibrant and free, filled with new ideas and the courage to go after them. No matter what your life looks like now, this is the time to begin stepping into your greatness . . . letting your light shine . . . going for it!

You may be thinking, "Are you kidding? You don't even know me. My life's a mess! My self-esteem is shot. How can I possibly live a life of freedom when I feel totally trapped in the life I have now?" I once said the same thing. Then I discovered that we're all set up to be as happy and free as we allow ourselves to be. I realized how often I stopped the flow of happiness . . . the joy of freedom, usually because I was afraid or because I thought I wasn't worth it. But you know what? As I took one tiny step forward at a time, even if my guts were churning and my knees were knocking, I discovered that I was worth it! So are you! We each have within us everything it takes to set ourselves free. One choice at a time, discover the beauty and the power that is you and then say yes to you!

You have more faith than you realize. Take a look at everyday actions like driving the car—when you approach the car it's with the expectation that the door will open (it's not jammed), you sit in the driver's seat (it won't give out under your weight), put on the seat belt (it will fit correctly), turn the key or push the button (it will work) and the car will start. You don't worry that each of these activities may or may not take place—you simply act on your basic belief that the car will start. There you have it—faith in action! *Freedom* is about reminding you that you already have the faith it takes to live the life you deserve to live—the life you were born to live.

P_AUSE FOR A MOMENT and think about the last hour. Were your thoughts mostly positive or mostly negative? If they were mostly negative because you have a lot to worry about, you now have a good place to begin. As you read through the messages in *Freedom... free to be me,* you'll discover that you're capable of turning those negative thoughts around. You'll start to see each worrisome situation through eyes of hope instead of hopeless resignation. The situation still exists, but your response to it is different—it no longer overwhelms you. The door to freedom has been opened a tiny bit, enough to sense the possibilities that exist on the other side. Once you know freedom is there for you, you can't un-know it. Something within you will gently urge you forward, and your life will begin to change.

The instant you make a new choice, you're in the process of transformation. As new choices accumulate, you'll discover that you are much more courageous and capable than you may have thought yourself to be. You'll find your self-esteem rising. One day at a time—sometimes one minute at a time—you'll realize that more positive thoughts have made their way into your very creative mind. The path to freedom well under way, you're beginning to choose to be the person you *want* to be. As the universe pays attention to the changes in you, it responds to those changes. You'll find that happier situations, people and events start showing up in your life. It feels great, and you're the one who's making it happen!

The door is now wide open for *you* to start showing up in your life—the real you—not the person you thought you had to be to make everyone else happy, or the person you believed yourself to be yesterday. You are free to be who you *really* are! Discovering what you like to do, the values that are important to you, and the dreams that are calling to you is a magnificent, transformative undertaking! *Your life is waiting for you.* Are you ready to embrace it?

Let *Freedom... free to be me* help be your conduit for change. There are several ways to enjoy *Freedom*.

- ♥ You can move through it sequentially, beginning with Day 1. After reading the first message, close your eyes and let it speak to you personally. You may journal about it or even draw what comes up for you. As your day progresses, let the message guide your thoughts and actions.

- ♥ If you have a challenge, or you want to read about a particular topic, *Freedom* has an Index in the back. Feel free to spend time contemplating the messages contained within a particular topic.

- ♥ It's always fun to close your eyes, open the book, and point to any place on the page. That becomes the message for your day!

- ♥ If you have a friend or prayer partner who is also reading *Freedom*, together you can discuss the message each of you has chosen for the day.

I went from atheist to believer because, at a low point in my life, I became open to a new possibility, seeing life through new eyes. Waiting for me was the God of my understanding, accepting me exactly as I was. Everything changed! With the guidance of my own inner wisdom, I found my courage and began living a life greater than I ever thought possible—a life of freedom. This book came from my personal experiences. Your experiences may be very different—they are uniquely yours. Hopefully, *Freedom* will help jump-start a whole new life for you, as you accept the freedom and happiness that you deserve. Is it easy? No. Is it worth it? Yes! *You* are worth it!

With love, respect, and appreciation,

Jane

Freedom...
free to be me

~ Day 1 ~

Making a difference

You'd be amazed if you knew how many lives have been touched in wonderful ways because they crossed paths with you. The smallest kindness can change a person's day, and sometimes it changes their whole outlook on life. That kind of thoughtfulness comes so naturally to you that you don't even notice you're offering it . . . but others notice. You really do make a difference.

I make a positive difference in the world, just by being me.

~ Day 2 ~

Choosing to have a good day

When my goal is to have a good day, I have a good day, no matter what it might look like on the outside. Lots of things can go "wrong" and I make them part of my good day. I can choose to be kind when someone is unkind or cheerfully patient when there's a need to wait. Deciding to have a good day brings out the best in me! The situation isn't nearly as important as my response to it. That's freedom!

When I choose to have a good day, I have a good day, no matter what it looks like on the outside.

~ DAY 3 ~

Letting go with love

I used to hold those I cared about tightly, trying to make sure we were all safe and happy. Then I remembered how much I had grown through my hardest challenges. Shouldn't I give them the same opportunity? How else will they know how capable they really are? I changed my focus from, "I have to save them," to "It's their chance to grow." Today I let go with love.

> *With love, I give others the dignity of growing through their own challenges.*

~ DAY 4 ~

Living the life I was born to live

If you surrender to the creative energy of the universe you will ride it. If you yield to love you will feel it. If you bow to wisdom you will know it. There's a most beautiful light shining in all of us! Trust the beauty of who you really are and allow anything unlike it to fall away. Stand tall, take a deep breath, and live the life you were born to live!

> *I stand tall, take a deep breath, and live the life I'm supposed to live!*

～ DAY 5 ～

Traffic lights are Love-reminders

Traffic lights are Love-reminders. Red = stop = rest. Put your feet up, do nothing for a while. It's okay to take a break! Yellow = slow down = take a walk. Notice what's around you and be grateful for what you see. Green = go = jump in! It's time to say yes to a life that sees your potential and knows your value. Take the next step and own the greatness that is you! Reminders to take care of ourselves are all around us!

When I'm sitting at a traffic light, I'll take the opportunity to remember all the ways I can take care of myself.

～ DAY 6 ～

Learning from my relationships

I recognize that every single person who has ever been in my life has been there for a reason. Within each relationship has been something for me to learn in order to grow into the person I want to be. Some have given me the courage to stand up for myself. Others have shown me the value of standing up for someone else. Each relationship helps me accept more completely, forgive more freely and love more fully.

With gratitude, I realize that every relationship helps me grow into the person I want to be.

~ Day 7 ~

I chart my life's course

I chart the course of my own life. In any given situation I can choose to be a victim or a champion. My choice affects my mood (miserable or empowered) and my reaction (defensive or open-minded). When my focus is on being the very best me I can be, it not only changes the way I feel, it takes me down a path paved with self-respect, strength and grace.

My choices chart the course of my life. Today I choose to be the best me I can be.

~ Day 8 ~

Detaching with love

Trying to change loved ones is crazy-making! How can I expect love or respect from someone who doesn't have love or respect to give? How fruitless is it to try to make them adhere to my point of view when I don't understand theirs? Today I acknowledge reality in my relationships. Coming from a place of acceptance I detach with love, setting us both free from my expectations.

Acknowledging reality in my relationships, I detach with love, setting us both free from my expectations.

~ Day 9 ~

Islands in the ocean

We're connected to each other by the greatest love of all, sharing the DNA of divine love. As we go about our daily lives we're like islands in the ocean—on the surface we appear to be separate, while underneath we're connected. With confidence the Creator gave us the free will to make our own decisions, to be our own unique selves. Thus, like magnificent islands, we're wonderfully distinctive in our own way while related by divine love at our core.

I am uniquely, wonderfully me, and at my core divine love connects me to everyone else.

~ Day 10 ~

I don't have to be perfect to move forward

There are many things I don't know, which invites me to stay teachable. The more patient I am as I learn something new, the easier the process. Sometimes I need to ask another person to help guide me through my learning curve. Their patience becomes a gift to me, a reminder that I don't have to be perfect to move forward.

I choose to stay teachable, knowing I don't have to be perfect to move forward.

~ DAY 11 ~

Paying attention

The Beloved is wherever you are, always and forever seeking your attention. Even when you're crazy-busy and your mind is trying to balance ten thoughts at once, a sudden sense of calm will weave its way into your consciousness. It's often a simple message like, 'Take a moment to breathe,' or 'There's plenty of time.' You ask, "Where did *that* come from?" Don't try to shake it off— it's time to pay attention.

> *No matter what I'm doing, even when I'm crazy-busy, the God of my understanding is there.*

~ DAY 12 ~

I'm worthy of my own self-respect

Love holds hands with distrust, allowing doubt to breathe easier. Kindness wraps its energy around cynicism, encouraging compassion and gentleness. Self-care caresses guilt and self-judgment, softening the effects of negativity turned inward. The light within each of us forever reminds us that we are worthy of our own self-respect.

> *No matter what my life feels and looks like, I'm worthy of my own self-respect.*

～ Day 13 ～

My awakening is personal to me

The process of awakening is personal to each. A walk in nature can trigger a truth from deep within us, reminding us of our connection with all things. For an instant, we absolutely know that we're all One. Our job is to recognize that this awareness is real, focus on it, experience its energy and sink into to the feeling of it, allowing it to change us.

My process of awakening is personal, and it changes me.

～ Day 14 ～

Giving myself permission to be happy

I give myself permission to be happy in this moment. Even if my life is turned upside down and I can't seem to find my footing, it's okay to be happy for this moment. Knowing I deserve happiness, I take a deep breath and feel that I'm alive. Whatever's going on will pass and things will get better. In the meantime I'll find moments of happiness, just because I can.

In this moment I take a deep breath and give myself permission to be happy.

~ Day 15 ~

I am always heard

When you turn to God in prayer, you are heard. When you rage at the circumstances of your life, you are heard. When your heart is heavy because of a loved one's pain, you are heard. When you can hardly contain your excitement about a new idea, you are heard. The God of your understanding knows you intimately, loves you completely, and always, always hears you.

When I turn to the God of my understanding in prayer, I am always heard.

~ Day 16 ~

Saying yes to my goals

How many times have I talked myself out of trying something new? I shouldn't apply for that job because so many more are better qualified? Why try to write a book when there are already millions of books on the market? In reality, I was writing 'failure' on my forehead! No more! Today I see what's right about me instead of comparing myself to others. I stand for my worth and say yes to my goals.

Today I see what's right about me. I stand for my worth and say yes to my goals.

～ DAY 17 ～

Good's going to come from this!

There have been times when a situation has knocked me off my feet. Because a positive attitude is important, I mentally grab hold of something to hang onto. I say, "Good's going to come from this—I just know it!" That becomes my affirmation, shifting my consciousness away from "Oh no!" into faith, igniting a light where before there was darkness.

In any challenge I say, "Good's going to come from this—I just know it!"

～ DAY 18 ～

Soothing myself

By giving ourselves the time and space to grieve the loss of a relationship, career, loved one, dream, or anything else important to us, we create the space for our feelings to be felt. Although it's tempting to stay busy to avoid the pain, it only pushes it below the surface where it's liable to pop up later in very uncomfortable ways. We're worth the time it takes right now to recognize, appreciate and soothe the parts of us that are hurting.

I'm worth the time it takes right now to soothe the parts of me that are hurting.

~ Day 19 ~

My soul is a lantern

My soul stands like a lantern, infiltrating its beam of hope through every messy life experience, "I'm here! Come this way! I'll guide you." Sensing its signal, I'm offered a pathway through the chaos. Once I take action, solutions begin to appear, seemingly out of nowhere! As Life makes the way possible, faith guides me by means of my own inner light.

> *When I don't know what to do, my own inner light stands ready to guide me.*

~ Day 20 ~

Letting go of regret

I endeavor to live my life without hanging onto regret. If I'm carrying around remorse from my past, I either forgive it (and myself) or I take action on it—righting a wrong or making amends. If I'm lamenting something that's happening today I do the same thing—dealing with it so as not to leave room for regret tomorrow. Life offers happiness. As I release any signs of regret, happiness becomes my choice.

> *There's no room in my life for regret. I deal with it and then let it go.*

~ Day 21 ~

Times of rest are creative

Times of rest are important as I move toward my goals, offering relaxation and rejuvenation for my mind and body. As my mind and body take a break, a space is created for fresh ideas to show up, along with new levels of excitement. As a creative being, my life is never stagnant. My times of rest are more than renewal—they're filled with creative possibility.

As I rest my mind and body, I create a space for new ideas.

~ Day 22 ~

Dropping the habit of worrying

Worry is a powerful force. It wrinkles our faces, our minds and our lives. Worrying about world affairs sends negative energy to the very situations we want to uplift. Worrying about our finances sends a message to the universe that money makes us feel bad. The best gift we can offer ourselves and the world is to drop the habit of worrying and replace it with optimism and faith.

I drop the habit of worrying and replace it with optimism and faith.

~ Day 23 ~

Discovering who I am

When I was a child the whole world was a curious mystery. As a young adult I tried to figure out what worked for me and what didn't—where did I fit? As an adult I had just enough knowledge to understand that experience is the greatest teacher. Now as an older adult I'm filled with gratitude for all of it, including the hardest challenges, as each experience brought me to who I am today.

As I realize how much I've learned from experience, I appreciate who I am today.

~ Day 24 ~

What if I knew my dream will come true?

If you knew without a doubt that your dream would come true you'd go for it, wouldn't you? So ask yourself, "What's stopping me?" If your hope is shaky because you've already tried, or the dream seems too big, know that it's still alive in you, waiting to be reactivated. The universe is poised to act on your behalf. With renewed commitment, one tiny step at a time, start again!

My dream is waiting to come true, and I'm going for it!

~ DAY 25 ~

Changing my mind

It's okay to change my mind. It's okay to leave the neighborhood, lifestyle, church or career that's been part of my life forever to go in a different direction. It's okay to explore new creative activities, nutrition choices, movie genres, travel adventures. Changing my mind expands my conscious awareness of the possibilities beckoning me today. It's not just okay, it's motivating!

Changing my mind is not just okay, it's motivating!

~ DAY 26 ~

Fear can lead to compassion

When I look back at the times I've been unhappy with myself, I can see that my behavior was rooted in fear—fear of rejection, being wrong, losing control of the situation. Today I remember that just like me, fear causes others to do things they would never do otherwise. With a new awareness, judgement falls away as I become open to understanding and compassion.

Remembering that fear has caused me to be unhappy with myself, I can offer understanding and compassion to others who are also afraid.

~ Day 27 ~

Putting forgiveness into perspective

Before she died my ninety-eight-year-old mom put forgiveness in perspective—she had no time for grudges. In her long lifetime, she learned that *her* happiness was what she could control. Fuming and fretting about others just wasn't worth it, no matter what they did. She set them free and got on with her life, with the perspective and choices she could control.

I have no time for grudges. I set others free and get on with creating my own happiness.

~ Day 28 ~

I am worthy, just as I am

When I have that feeling in the pit of my stomach that asks, "Are you about to say something that's trying to prove your worth?" it's a huge red flag. The Beloved has taught me that I am worthy, period. Thinking I need to prove it means I'm either with the wrong person, in the wrong situation, and/or I'm thinking wrongly about it. My job is to figure out what's true and act accordingly.

I am worthy, just as I am. I have no need to prove it.

~ DAY 29 ~

I can choose a new beginning

I can choose a new beginning! Instead of seeing a circumstance from the knee-jerk negative reactions of my old thinking, I can see it in a brand new light filled with optimism. I proclaim, "I know this situation is somehow *for* me. I'll look for the good in it, I'll find ways to be grateful, and I'll be the most beautiful ME I can possibly be in it!" And it is—a new beginning is born!

I can choose a new beginning filled with gratitude and optimism.

~ DAY 30 ~

The truth within me

When I'm disappointed in myself, when I'm frightened for a loved one, when I can't even imagine world peace, there is a place deep within me that knows the truth for all of us. Noticing my breath and the beating of my heart, I lean into that place, surrendering my human worries to the One. I stay there until finally, I feel Love fill me. I'm ready to begin again.

No matter what's happening, I'm renewed by the truth within me.

~ Day 31 ~

Sharing my gift of love

Love is our nature and giving is how we share it. A gift we can all give is to leave someone feeling better about themselves because they've been in our presence. A kind word, a listening ear, a smile or a bit of patience helps others know that they are seen and valued. They matter in the world. When we share our gifts we uplift everyone, including ourselves!

I share my gift of love by leaving others feeling better because they've been in my presence.

~ Day 32 ~

Success notebook

It's helpful to keep a notebook filled with small, everyday successes. Every time you complete even the smallest project, take a risk, make that phone call, set a boundary, or stand up for yourself, make a note of it. Those entries go a long way to erase doubt when it starts to creep in, and it sets the stage for your next success. After all, you have a long track record of success!

My success notebook reminds me of how successful I am!

~ Day 33 ~

Nature's wisdom

Nature reminds me of what's possible. If trees know when to let go of dying leaves so that new ones can emerge, I can let go of negativity to make room for peace and joy. If birds can fly hundreds of miles to fulfill their life's purpose, I can take the next step to live my dreams. Teachers are everywhere! With appreciation, I notice and follow their example.

With appreciation, I notice Nature's wisdom and learn from her example.

~ Day 34 ~

An attitude of gratitude

Propelled by negative beliefs of "I don't have enough," money was limited. My focus on lack brought on more lack! Today I have new beliefs based on an attitude of gratitude! I'm grateful for what I already have. I'm grateful for my restraint in spending. I'm grateful for my bills and pay them gladly. Gratitude helped me dump old beliefs and welcome financial security.

With an attitude of gratitude, I say yes to prosperity.

~ Day 35 ~

Setting boundaries for myself

I respect myself enough to set boundaries for *me*. My time is precious, and I get to choose how I'll spend it. If I'm not uplifted by what I'm doing, I'm sending a message to the universe that it's okay for me to be less than happy and fulfilled. If what I'm doing is right for me, it sends a message that I value myself. Setting healthy personal boundaries is good for me!

> *Setting healthy personal boundaries values me, and I'm worth it!*

~ Day 36 ~

When death is imminent

My mom lived in an assisted living facility and I spent time with her daily. One day a woman at the facility passed away. The lady's best friend, who had been struggling with her pal's decline, intuitively knew it was time to go see her. She was grateful to find her friend quietly serene, and within a few hours she died. Paying attention to our own inner wisdom can bring peace and comfort for both the living and dying.

> *I lean into my own inner wisdom, creating a place for peace and comfort for the living and the dying.*

~ Day 37 ~

Willingness before action

Willingness sets a solid foundation for action. In Al-Anon I became willing to make amends to those I had harmed before I actually spoke to anyone—it paved the way for the honesty, humility, courage, and respect needed to take responsibility for my choices. Once I became willing, following through was easier. In the process I learned that I was worthy of change.

Willingness sets me up for the action that shows me I'm worthy of change.

~ Day 38 ~

Quantum physics

The science of quantum physics explains that everything is energy—waves of possibility—until it's observed. Once observed, the waves collapse into particles, and form is created. When I pay attention to anything, positive or negative, I'm observing it and causing it to collapse into form. The results are my life experiences. If my thoughts are mostly positive, I have mostly positive experiences. If they're mostly negative, I have mostly negative experiences. Today I'm mindful of where I focus my attention.

I focus on what makes me happy, which invites more happiness into my life.

~ Day 39 ~

Growing from each life experience

I love the way sidewalks make way for creation by allowing a crack to develop. Then a tiny seed takes hold in the earth below, a plant growing strong enough to poke its head up through the opening to say, "Hello! I'm here!" I can learn a lot from the crack in the sidewalk *and* the seed that grows from it! I grow stronger from each life experience, stretching and expanding, gaining confidence, breaking through to show up and live life to the fullest.

> *I grow stronger from each life experience, showing up to live life to the fullest.*

~ Day 40 ~

Aha!

Have you ever had an "Aha! I'm courageous!" experience? It's the one where you notice, "Look what I just did!" Even if you didn't do the scary thing well, at least you did it, and that's empowering! Doing it well can come later. The empowering high comes from the willingness to do it the first time. We've all had first steps. We're all courageous. Good for us!

> *I notice and appreciate every "Aha! I'm courageous!" experience, no matter what it looks like.*

~ DAY 41 ~

Accepting happiness

The door to happiness is never closed—it's ours to open, even when life feels hard. Every positive thought, each kindness to our self or another, opens the door to happiness and changes the course of our lives. The more we realize we're worthy of happiness, the more willing we become to accept it. After a while, that happiness door is wide open and the sunshine of joy floods in!

I'm worthy of happiness, and I accept it!

~ DAY 42 ~

The energy of love

The divine energy of love is present in the sunlight and in the shadows. It's easy to sense the God that adores us in the sunlight, when the world is beautiful and all is well. The greatest blessing comes in discovering its comfort, strength and peace in the shadows, where it holds us in the energy of its embrace until we remember that no matter what's happening, we are its beloved one.

The divine energy of love is in the shadows of my life,
holding me as I remember that I'm its beloved one.

~ Day 43 ~

My spiritual path belongs to me

Ever since I discovered that God is real I've upset a few apple carts. Some people were less than happy as I began to walk away from activities and discussions that I used to participate in. Instead of feeling guilty, I learned not to feel bad because of other people's upset. Instead I'm responsible for my own spiritual path, which is new and exciting—the perfect path for me!

As my spiritual path changes the way I move through life, I gratefully let go of the old to follow the path that's perfect for me.

~ Day 44 ~

Beginnings and endings

Beginnings take time as I learn how to navigate my "new normal." Endings also take time. They can make me feel vulnerable, adrift in "What am I supposed to do now?" In reality, the ending is a new beginning, filled with possibility. Knowing that I live in a friendly universe that wants only my highest happiness, I gather my courage and gratefully begin my life's next chapter.

Knowing that every ending is really a new beginning, I gratefully begin the next chapter of my story.

～ Day 45 ～

My contentment is a blessing

Quantum Physics tells us that everything is energy, including us. Therefore, I contribute to the collective energy of the universe. If I spend the day deliciously happy with my nose in a good book, my pet curled up beside me, I contribute peace, joy and serenity to the universe. I don't have to be doing something "constructive" to contribute—the vibration of my contented energy is a blessing.

I happily take breaks from the busy-ness of life. My contentment is a blessing to the world.

～ Day 46 ～

Healing pain-buttons

If someone continually pushes the buttons that trigger old pain, I can learn from it. My pain-button tells me there's a soft spot within me that hasn't yet healed. If I continue to allow that person to push my buttons, it's like picking a scab so that the injury can't heal. Freedom comes from making my healing more important than the behavior I've allowed in the past. Perhaps it's time to set a boundary while I do the work to un-install the pain-button that exists.

Healthy boundaries give me the time and space to un-install the pain-button that exists.

~ Day 47 ~

I'm stronger than I believe myself to be

Challenges are part of the human condition—everyone has overcome something. Overcoming challenges is hard work—frustrating, humbling, exhausting, often embarrassing—and at the same time empowering. Working through difficulties shines a light on the possibilities waiting on the other side. In the process we discover we're stronger than we knew. Good for us for making it through!

Overcoming challenges teaches me that I'm strong. Kudos to me for making it through!

~ Day 48 ~

I'm changing all the time

Nothing stays the same—including me! I'm not the same person today than I was five years ago, or even a year ago. The thoughts and beliefs that were true for me then aren't necessarily true for me now. Peeling away the old fears and hurts, I'm finding someone new with fresh ideas and interests. With gratitude, I let go of the old and shine the light of the person I am today!

I'm changing all the time! As I let go of the old, I shine the light of light of the person I am today.

~ DAY 49 ~

Leaving mistakes behind

I pray for a world in which we all dance to the gentle wisdom of Love's message. Divine love reminds us to clean up the baggage our mistakes have made and then leave the mistake behind—get on with life! Know that others are doing the same. What may look a bit like chaos is really all of us taking responsibility for our lives and then getting on with living them. It's a messy, sacred process.

Taking responsibility, I clean up the baggage my mistakes have made and then get on with my life.

~ DAY 50 ~

People who believe in me

I practice self-care by surrounding myself with people who believe in me. They care about me when my mood is up and when it's not. I can have fun with them and lean on them when needed. It's reciprocal—I stand by them the same way. These relationships help me grow in both giving and receiving with a full, open heart. Today I choose my relationships wisely.

Surrounding myself with people who believe in me, I learn about giving and receiving with a full, open heart.

~ Day 51 ~

Simple, everyday successes

Something special happens as you get older—you have the ability to look back at your life and see how much you've changed. You've done a lot of learning! You can also see to what extent you've made a difference in the world. How many people have been uplifted because they came into your presence, if just for a moment? To me, those are simple, everyday successes!

With joy and gratitude I look back at the simple, everyday successes in my life.

~ Day 52 ~

Opening my heart

At one point the world seemed like a hard place. After getting hurt enough times I hardened my heart, closing myself off so I wouldn't be hurt again. The problem was that I lost out on the joy of life's beauty. The answer was to open my heart again. When the old pain surfaced, I softly breathed into it. My softened heart filled with compassion and I saw the world through new eyes.

I open my heart to see with new, compassionate eyes.

~ DAY 53 ~

Self-discovery in solitude

Being on a spiritual path often invites solitude as a means of self-discovery. On my path I've learned that 'being alone' and 'being lonely' are two entirely different states of mind. Loneliness brings up sadness and rejection, while solitude is a choice that invites privacy and peace. Within the quiet of my alone time, I relax into the discovery of the beauty of who I truly am.

> *Solitude is the choice I make to discover the beauty of who I truly am.*

~ DAY 54 ~

Self-sabotage

There have been times when I've come close to reaching a goal only to sabotage success. I want to exercise but tell myself I'm too tired or too busy. I want to volunteer but hesitate at the commitment. The self-sabotage becomes an excuse that ultimately robs me of my goal. I turn to my inner wisdom to help me love myself enough to accept the good that Life is offering and move toward my goals.

> *I love myself enough to accept the good that Life is offering and go for it!*

~ Day 55 ~

Non-action is an option

Sometimes non-action is the best option. When I'm feeling vulnerable and unsure of myself, my best course of action is to let go of the need to make something happen. This isn't the time to make hasty decisions solely to make myself feel better. Instead I choose to pause, mindfully letting this period unfold. When it's time, I'll know what to do and how to take the first step.

When non-action is the best option, I pause and wait until I know how to move forward.

~ Day 56 ~

Peace is a full-time job

My prayer is that someday we'll have peace on earth. My job is to be a place of peace today. When I'm standing in line, get cut off on the freeway or find myself in the middle of family drama, how will I respond? How would peace respond? That's what I must do. If I'm not willing to be peaceful in my own life, how can I expect it in the world? World peace is a personal, full-time job.

When life doesn't go my way, I choose to be a place of peace.

~ Day 57 ~

The ripple effect of kindness

Have you ever had one of those days when you feel blah, moving on auto-pilot without fully engaging in anything? Then one person catches your attention with a kind word, a smile, or a comment that makes you laugh. It begins a ripple effect that shakes loose the doldrums. Once again, things look brighter. Suddenly you remember that life can be wonderful!

As I give or receive kindness, I become part of the ripple effect that brightens the world.

~ Day 58 ~

I'm part of the solution

How many times I have wished a problem would just go away! Although I may want the easy way out, it doesn't work like that because I'm part of the solution. In order for a problem to go away I have to address it. If money is a struggle, or I'm not sleeping well or I have indigestion, it's my job to discover why and take responsible action. Once I pinpoint the problem, I create a space where solutions can make themselves known. It reminds me of just how powerful I am.

When I'm wishing that a problem would just go away, I remember that I'm part of the solution.

~ Day 59 ~

Unconditional love

The God that adores me also cherishes those who are so filled with fear and self-condemnation that their words and actions hurt others and themselves. The Beloved never gives up on us, meeting every single thought, word and act with unconditional love. Sometimes that love is felt and change is initiated . . . and sometimes not. Either is okay—that's how unconditional love works.

> *No matter what I think, say or do, I'm loved unconditionally by a God that adores me.*

~ Day 60 ~

I choose healthy relationships

Because everything is energy, it's important to notice how I feel when I'm around certain people. Is the energy free-flowing and uplifting, or does it slow down? Everyone's path is perfect for them, but not everyone's path is perfect for me. Noticing my choices, Life gives me more of what I accept for myself. Following my intuition, I choose relationships that are healthy for me.

> *What I accept for myself is what Life will give to me. I choose healthy relationships.*

~ Day 61 ~

Looking for the gift

I trust that what's around the corner is always for me, even though I have no idea what it will be. The God that adores me would not bring something or someone into my life that doesn't contain a gift. If it looks like a challenge and I can't see the gift, it's my opportunity to adjust my focus. As I start looking for the good in it—believing that it's there—the whole experience changes!

I see every situation as a gift and start looking for the good in it. It changes the whole experience!

~ Day 62 ~

Curiosity paves the way

I have a hunch that curiosity is the Beloved's way of inching us forward. We go down one path to discover what it has to offer, and that path shows us just enough to spark more interest. Because we humans are a curious bunch, we keep investigating . . . trying things out . . . making changes to see what happens. In the process we discover that the world is filled with amazing possibilities!

As my curiosity is ignited I keep inching forward, discovering amazing possibilities for my life!

~ Day 63 ~

Doing what I love to do

There's a lot to be said about doing what I love to do. When I'm doing something I love to do, it's harder for my buttons to get pushed—why change my good mood? I'm less apt to try to control others when I'm immersed in my own joyous activity. It's much easier to stay calm if a sudden challenge occurs because my mind is open and free as I do my own thing. Just imagine what might happen if we all practiced doing the activities we love!

The world is a whole lot brighter when I'm doing what I love to do.

~ Day 64 ~

Standing in my own truth

Freedom is born the moment you stand in your own truth, no matter what everyone else is doing around you. If you're at a gathering that's become uncomfortable, it's the moment you decide to leave. If your friends are going to an event you know you can't afford, it's the moment when you decide to stay home. The moments may seem small, but their significance is huge.

As I stand in my own truth, my freedom is born.

~ Day 65 ~

My thoughts about today

Today will not be any better than my thoughts about it. My mind is full of thoughts, some of them helpful and some not so much. Will I rant about traffic, the news and family drama, filling my mind with judgement and anger, or will I accept life just as it is, without getting caught up in how it should be? I get to decide what kind of a day I will have. It begins with my thoughts about it.

Today won't be any better than my thoughts about it. I choose my thoughts wisely.

~ Day 66 ~

Asking for help

Asking for help isn't easy for many. Try looking at it this way: Have you ever had a friend call you because they just needed to talk or they're sick or injured and need groceries, a ride to the doctor or some of your homemade soup? Remember how good it felt to be asked? The next time you're lonely, sick, frightened, or need help in any way, I hope you'll remember how good it feels to be asked. Then ask for help—it's a win-win for both!

When it's time for me to ask for help, I'll remember the benefits for both .

~ DAY 67 ~

When do I reach out?

How are we to know if and when we should reach out to someone who seems to be heading in an unhealthy direction? Do I say something? Our intuition is contained within the wisdom of our soul, and it's always available. With a question as simple as, 'What do I do in this situation?' we're guided as to what to say, when to say it and when to say nothing. Our job is to listen and follow.

When I don't know when to reach out to another, there's a part of me that does know.

~ DAY 68 ~

A prayer for comfort

Dear Beloved One,
On this day I pray that those who are hurting feel your comfort, the frightened realize their strength, and the angry awaken to inner peace. Hold us all so fully in your love that we understand that we are worthy, cherished and safe. Your love is so big that it contains and heals us all, and for this I am grateful.

Within my prayer for comfort, I feel the strength and love of the One that cherishes us all.

~ Day 69 ~

The world is filled with heroes

People who listen to others with their full attention are heroes. So are devoted pet owners, recyclers, the person who holds the door for you, friends who notice when you could use a hug, and anyone who offers a smile or kind word. The world is filled with heroes—we've all been one and we've felt the benefits of being around one. Heroes abound!

I've benefitted from the heroes around me and I've been a hero. The world is filled with heroes!

~ Day 70 ~

Turning negativity around

We would think that our thoughts are secret, but they aren't really. They show up on our faces, in the way we move through the world, and in the way life responds to us. When I'm a mess, I take my negativity to the Beloved and dump it there, where it's safe. I no longer need to carry it around with me. In the process the Beloved reminds me of my lovability. With self-love in my pocket I pick myself up, choose a positive new thought and get on with my life.

When needed, I give my negativity to the God of my understanding, where it's safe. Then I choose a positive new thought and get on with my life.

~ Day 71 ~

The energy of peace

Peace is alive, a living energy that unites you and me, the family down the street, the rocks, the rivers and the fishes that live in them. We all have within us the ability to dip into the wellspring of the peace that is at our core . . . all of us. We are one magnificent manifestation of the Creator, and peace is our nature. As I move through my day, I let the energy of my peace be felt by all.

The energy of peace unites me with all creation. The energy of my peace is felt by all.

~ Day 72 ~

Letting go is for *me*

Letting go can be a very private thing. I don't need to work up to it, tell anyone or ask for advice. Instead I just know when the time is right. I let go of timeworn stories and resentments, much like retiring a tattered pair of old shoes. I let go of complaining because I choose to smile instead. In my decision to let go I discover the power of my own worth.

Letting go is a decision that I make for <u>me</u>. In the process I discover the power of my own worth.

~ DAY 73 ~

God's miracle

I wasn't born to fit in. I'm supposed to unleash the miracle of who I am, shining my own inner light. It can be daunting, but I'm finding out how courageous I can be. Not everyone will understand me. That's okay. I'm here to live my life, not to have everyone understand it. Fitting in doesn't work anymore. Becoming God's miracle is my mission, and I'm going for it!

With courage and commitment, I become the miracle of who I am.

~ DAY 74 ~

Letting my dream work with me

Trying to ask your dream to quit calling to you is like telling your heart to stop beating. You are meant to be happy, fulfilled, prosperous and free. Your dream awaits, offering you the joy you seek. What's keeping you from it? Asking for help to get started? Then ask. More skills? Sign up to take a class. Don't be the one to hold back—let your dream work with you as you move toward success.

I take the steps to let my dream work with me—a set-up for success!

~ DAY 75 ~

Families

There are all kinds of families—those we're born into, adopted into, marry into, partner into, join by association, and those we consciously create. The minute I bring home a pet, I've created a family. When I make the decision to surround myself with people who love and respect me for who I am, I create a family. It's my life. I gratefully embrace my choices.

I gratefully embrace my family choices. I'm worthy of love and respect.

~ DAY 76 ~

Fear is part of our human experience

Love leads the way through fear. Knowing that fear is part of the human experience, the Beloved offers its hand as I deal with it. It gives me a safe place to rest when I feel overwhelmed. Once I'm ready, Love helps me to my feet so I can take the next step. Then it walks with me, reminding me that faith and courage are also a part of the human experience.

Knowing that fear is part of my human experience, I walk through it with the God of my understanding.

∼ Day 77 ∼

Tears of grief

Tears of grief tell a silent story of the love and caring we have for another. Our tears are an outward expression of the sorrow deep within us, a sign of our loss. Such pain allows compassion to well up as a sacred part of who we are. It connects us with those who see our tears and bear witness to our sorrow, "I see you. I hear you. I stand beside you."

In times of grief I let my tears fall. I'm connected with the compassion of others.

∼ Day 78 ∼

My gifts are meant to be shared

Let nothing stop you from believing in your own worth and the talents that come with it. Divine love planted the ideas into your heart about the gifts you are to bring to the world, igniting your curiosity and excitement. You wouldn't have been given these dreams if you weren't capable of bringing them into fruition. In fact, you were specially chosen! Take the next step and say yes!

I was given my dreams on purpose. I was chosen to use my talents to bring them to fruition. Today I say yes!

~ DAY 79 ~

Discovering my strength

As we move forward on our spiritual path, some people become uncomfortable with the changes in us. They used to understand us, but now they're not so sure. It's an opportunity to discover the strength of who we're becoming, just like the caterpillar's transformation within the chrysalis, growing strong to become the butterfly. In our changes, we're growing strong to shine the beauty, truth and glory of who we are today.

My spiritual path is one of change. I discover the strength of who I'm becoming.

~ DAY 80 ~

My happiness is up to me

My life got a whole lot easier once I realized it's not anyone else's job to make me happy. In any situation, I can be as okay as I allow myself to be. If the circumstances aren't what I would have chosen I can ask: *What am I supposed to learn from this,* or *how can I have this situation be answered prayer?* Then I pay attention to *my* thoughts, *my* actions, *my* responses, and *my* growth. My happiness is up to me.

My happiness is up to me. In any situation, I pay attention to my thoughts, my actions, my responses, and my growth.

～ Day 81 ～

No or maybe?

If I really want to say NO, I've learned not to say MAYBE to keep from disappointing the other person or to keep the peace. MAYBE creates clutter in my head. It hangs out like an ominous cloud—I can't push it away. I know that eventually I'm going to have to say NO or cave in and do something I really don't want to do. MAYBE just prolongs the decision. NO gives the sun a chance to shine!

If I really want to say no, I say NO instead of MAYBE.

～ Day 82 ～

Taking a new path

Our spiritual journey is ultimately a solo one. We may start out with others of like mind, but sometimes there's an impetus to grow in a new direction, away from the group. There's no need to feel guilty, ask for permission, or to stay behind to keep the status quo. It's okay to sense a new path and follow it, trusting that the way will be made known.

My spiritual path belongs to me, and it's okay to step away from the group to follow it.

~ Day 83 ~

God-energy

It's easy to believe that living things like animals and plants have God-energy. Years ago I stood in an elevator by myself, touched its walls and could feel its energy. Then I sensed the divine message, "Yes, I am here." The Beloved was the elevator! Since then I've had that experience many times with countless 'things.' Now I know without a doubt that the Infinite One is in all things, at all times, in all places.

> *The God of my understanding is in all things, at all times, in all places.*

~ Day 84 ~

What do I allow?

If I'm less than happy, I need to give some thought as to what I'm allowing into my mind. Am I keen on keeping up with world news? Does it uplift me or leave me worried, frustrated and fearful? What might happen if I only spend a few minutes checking the headlines, and then say a prayer for world peace? Next I read something that puts a smile on my face or fills me with hope! I'm at choice as to where I put my focus.

> *I decide what to allow into my mind. Because the choice is mine, I gratefully make adjustments where needed.*

~ DAY 85 ~

Changing my mind is okay

Yesterday I changed my mind. I had agreed to do something several months ago and was excited about it, but with more recent information I realized it wasn't a match for me. With absolute appreciation for the other person, I lovingly and respectfully opted out. Most of all, I felt respect and appreciation for myself for changing my mind and doing something about it.

Changing my mind is always an option and reminds me that I'm worthy of my own self-respect.

~ DAY 86 ~

Letting go of my story

Forgiving myself and others happens when I'm no longer hooked into my story. I've stopped telling it. I no longer have the need to explain, defend, or make anyone wrong. It's simply done . . . in the past . . . complete. What's left is what I've learned from it. Taking the lessons forward, I'm stronger and wiser for the experience. Forgiveness allows me to be fully present in my life today.

As I let go of the need to defend my story, I am fully present in the beauty of today.

~ Day 87 ~

When challenges occur

When challenges occur, turning toward divine love is my answer—it opens the floodgates of limitless possibilities that my human mind can't see. I quit focusing on the problem, turn it over to the Beloved, and get on with my day. Sure enough, in the middle of a completely different activity, a great idea pops into my head! Love's work, no doubt . . .

> *When challenges occur I turn them over to the God of my understanding, making space for solutions to present themselves.*

~ Day 88 ~

Coloring outside the lines

Nature is Mother Nature's example of the infinite creativity within all of us. Look at what she's done with the combinations of shapes, colors, sizes and textures that are all around us—sunsets, flowers, birds and animals! That same creativeness offers us the ability to birth the life of our dreams. Today I'm free to color outside the lines of my own conventional thinking. I color in bright shades of joy, passion, freedom and love!

> *I'm free to color outside the lines—just think of what could be possible!*

~ Day 89 ~

Generosity

Gratitude opens up doors to the abundance of Life's goodness. A feeling of gratitude prompts generosity toward others as we share our listening ear, our time, ideas, laughter, respect, and forgiveness. Our generosity reminds us of the many ways we already have enough . . . that we already *are* enough. As our feelings of well-being grow, our generous hearts expand.

My gratitude opens the door to generosity. As I share from my generous heart, I expand my feeling of well-being.

~ Day 90 ~

Inner stirrings

When I look back on it, I opened the door to the God of my understanding when I turned fifty and asked, "Is this it? Is this all there is to my life?" My life wasn't horrible—it just wasn't enough. There was a stirring inside that said, "Hey, it's time for you! Put yourself first for a change!" Paying attention, I acted on it, and divine love was waiting.

I pay attention to the stirrings within me. I act on their message.

~ Day 91 ~

Standing tall in my integrity

I value the freedom to stand tall in my integrity, liking who I am. If I'm tempted to negatively react to someone else's comments or actions I ask myself, "Is the confrontation of right-fighting, even in my own mind, worth giving up the integrity that I stand for today?" No way! I choose to be the person I want to be, one conscious decision at a time.

In any situation, I'm free to stand tall in my integrity, choosing to be the person I want to be.

~ Day 92 ~

Letting go of fixing

Before I knew God was real I was very busy trying to fix those I cared about. That changed as I learned to listen to my own inner guidance. I asked, "What's mine to do?" Ninety percent of the time the answer was, "Do nothing. This doesn't belong to you." At first it was hard not to jump into fixing mode, but soon I learned to let go and relax. Life became so much easier when I realized I didn't need to control every situation!

When I'm tempted to try to fix someone else I ask, "What's mine to do?" Then I know how to proceed.

~ DAY 93 ~

Success and failure

A deep feeling of inner satisfaction comes with success, reminding us of what's right about us instead of what's wrong. Equally important is how we view failure, the other side of the success coin. When we see mistakes as a natural part of the growth process, we appreciate the learning that takes place at every level. Both sides of the coin are meant to be celebrated!

Knowing that success and failure are two sides of the same coin, I learn from each, appreciating all parts of myself.

~ DAY 94 ~

Taking a chance

In the past there have been times when an unexpected opportunity has presented itself. It catches me off-guard and I hesitate to jump in, even though my intuition tells me it's in my best interest. Today I know the occasion is a gift from a loving universe, conspiring for my happiness. It's a set-up moment pregnant with meaning, a chance to make a difference, to know myself more fully. Today I'm better at saying yes.

When my intuition tells me it's right, I take a chance and step into new opportunities.

~ Day 95 ~

Courage to be happy

It takes courage to be happy. It takes courage to turn your back on the old tapes playing in your head that list the reasons why you shouldn't be happy. It takes courage to believe that you live in a friendly universe that stands ready to support you as you move toward your next adventure. Ready, get set, go! Embrace your courage today and discover a whole new world created just for you!

I have the courage to let go of my old stuff and say yes to the happiness I deserve!

~ Day 96 ~

One hundred percent available

Deep, abiding peace is one hundred percent available to the family arguing at the dinner table, the driver honking their horn in traffic, and the person who just received a scary diagnosis from their doctor. The God of your understanding is just as awake, attentive and available at the dinner table, in your car and at doctor's office as it is in sitting in church or walking in nature.

No matter what's happening, the God of my understanding is one hundred percent available to me.

~ Day 97 ~

Looking at old beliefs

When an old fear-based belief resurfaces *again*, even though it's disturbing, it's a good thing! It tells me that I'm ready to look at it again because I'm spiritual stronger than I was the last time I addressed it. Consciously I ask, "Do I want to bring that past belief into the present moment? Do I want it to create tomorrow's experiences?" Thoughtfully I make my decisions and then I act on them.

Old beliefs come up because I'm spiritually ready to look at them again.

~ Day 98 ~

Learning from pets

Have you ever watched a cat by the window, their body warmed by the sun's rays? Have you noticed how dogs seem to find fun everywhere, whether it's chasing a stick, a ball, or their own tail? Animals have a lot to teach us about enjoying life—finding pleasure in the moment, just because it feels good! Our teachers are all around us, including those with four legs.

As I watch pets enjoy life by finding pleasure in the moment, it reminds me that I can do the same.

~ DAY 99 ~

Radiance of my own wisdom

Our holy journey—the one that's right for us—is within our own heart. Often another's insights help begin our path of inner discovery, but we are the only one who can sense our own light, learn to listen to its message, and shine the radiance of our own wisdom. We can then share our gifts with others on their journey, as they discover the truth for themselves within their own heart.

I sense the message of my own inner wisdom and shine the radiance of my own light.

~ DAY 100 ~

No playing small!

Every time you play small to appease someone else, your self-worth diminishes. Not standing up for yourself sends a powerful message to the universe that says, "I don't deserve happiness, fulfillment, peace." Is playing small to pacify another worth a lack of prosperity, fewer happy relationships, career struggles or a body that's not vibrantly healthy? No way! It's time to let yourself be seen and heard!

No playing small for me! I'm letting myself be seen and heard!

~ Day 101 ~

Hurtful words

There are many reasons why I may harbor ill will against another. Perhaps they talked behind my back, spreading untrue rumors about me. Triggering memories of past humiliation, including those still aching from childhood, it's easy to see why I would entertain defensive retribution. Today I have a new response. Standing in my own integrity, I'm free to let others have their say without any need to respond. I'm worthy of my own peace of mind.

When I've been triggered by someone else's words, I am free to let it go without any need to respond.

~ Day 102 ~

Painful feelings as teachers

The angst of worry, self-doubt and anger are great teachers. Even though it's uncomfortable, I've learned to lean into painful feelings to see what they can teach me. When I'm open and receptive to the lesson, the negative feeling has accomplished its goal and is released. I then have no need to re-learn that lesson. Feelings are temporary. The faith I have in life and in myself are forever.

I allow my painful feelings to teach me what I need to know, and then I release them.

~ Day 103 ~

Healing in giving

We all have something to give. In fact, giving can be a great path to healing. Giving compassion and understanding to another reminds us that if we can share it, we must have it within us to share. If we have it within us, then surely we can offer it to ourselves. Our greatest healing comes from believing that we are worth that which we offer to others.

I heal myself by believing that I'm worth the compassion and understanding I offer to others.

~ Day 104 ~

My full potential

The majesty of the plant is within the seed. Nourished by water, sun, soil and air, it grows to its full potential. The majesty of the butterfly is within the caterpillar. Nurtured by its transformation within the chrysalis, it grows to its full potential. The majesty of the Creator is within us. Nurtured by conscious awareness within each human experience, we grow to our full potential.

As I consciously move through each life experience, I grow to my full potential.

~ Day 105 ~

My enough-ness

The moment I understood the Beloved's promise that I really am good enough, everything changed. The awareness didn't feel self-centered or arrogant—instead it was an "Aha!" moment with the full understanding that I don't have to prove myself. We are all enough, just as we are. Even if we never change anything about ourselves, we are loved unconditionally in our enough-ness. All is well.

I don't have to prove myself—I am enough just as I am.

~ Day 106 ~

Smiling for no reason

Some days I make the decision to smile for no reason—just because! On those days I'm more apt to notice the good that's around me. I chuckle at unexpected delights like squirrels chasing each other, the sun peeking out from behind a cloud, a corny joke or my own goofiness. Looking for good, I find it! Today is such a day.

Today's a very good day to smile for no reason, delighting at the good around me!

~ Day 107 ~

The feeling of my dream opens doors

When I ruminate about reaching my dreams, doubt creeps in. Then I turn to my own inner wisdom—my personal cheerleader. I'm reminded that I don't need to figure out how to make the dream happen on my own—the universe lends a helping hand. While I act on the *feeling* of my dream—what's alive in my heart—the universe notices and doors start to open to help make it happen!

> *As I focus and act on the feeling of my dream, the universe opens doors toward its fulfillment.*

~ Day 108 ~

Letting my life speak for itself

Sometimes you just have to let your actions speak for themselves. To my mom it made no sense when I retired as minister of my church to spread my message beyond its walls. "What about stability, finances?" Within a few months my first book, *Choices: choosing me is OK,* was published. Mom saw how happy I was. She ordered a couple of copies. When they arrived we looked at them together, and we both had tears in our eyes. I think she understood. It was a pretty special moment.

> *When others don't understand my actions, I can simply let my life speak for itself.*

~ Day 109 ~

Sharing a secret with myself

If you're getting ready for an event or situation that's making you nervous, consider sharing a little secret with yourself. Wear your wildest underwear to that serious meeting, slide your lucky charm into your pocket before going to the interview, mail yourself a congratulations card for a job well done, and plan a special treat for yourself at the end of the day. You're worth your most positive encouragement!

When something's making me nervous, I share a little secret with myself, knowing I'm worth my most positive encouragement.

~ Day 110 ~

The love at my core

The divine love that created us lives at our core, a wellspring of love that bubbles up and overflows in every direction. As we give love, our core-love grows and multiplies. That's the way it works. Ultimately, learning to love ourselves is the greatest gift we can offer ourselves and the world. The more we believe that love begins with ourselves, the easier it is to share it with others.

When I love myself, the love at my core multiplies, allowing me to share love with everyone and everything around me.

~ Day 111 ~

Prosperity starts with me

The Beloved taught me that prosperity starts with me. First I had to believe that I'm worth it. The abundance of the universe was hovering, waiting to plop its bounty into my lap once I let go of my "not good enough" thinking. So I listened to the wisdom of my soul and I learned of my worth. As I started to believe that I was deserving of life's goodness, everything else began to take care of itself, including my finances.

I accept the prosperity that is mine, knowing that I'm worthy of the bounty of the universe.

~ Day 112 ~

Letting my imagination fly

Kids are uninhibited about creating. As a teacher, sometimes I'd load tables with touchy-feely inventive items and art materials. The kid's assignment was to let loose their imagination and create . . . period. The process was glorious! We ended up with a joyous potpourri of ideas brought to life in form! We all have a child within us, so go for it—soar!

With joy I let my imagination fly, bringing to life the ideas within me.

~ Day 113 ~

Starting my day with prayer

I'm grateful to begin my day with prayer. How I pray makes no difference—there's no right or wrong. It's simply one way that I connect with a God that's real to me. Within my prayer I remember that no matter what the day brings, I'm not alone. I'm held in grace in every conversation I have with others, and especially in the conversations I have with myself. Starting the day with prayer reminds me that I am loved, I am safe, and I'm never alone.

I start my day with prayer as a reminder that what wherever I am, whatever I'm doing, I'm not alone.

~ Day 114 ~

Taking action

You learn to trust yourself by taking action. Sometimes the action is big, but more often it's in smaller, everyday activities. When you make the decision to donate the clothes you no longer wear, you not only honor the clothes and the person who will enjoy them next, you also honor yourself. By letting go of what no longer serves you, you set into motion a brand new, joyous life! Doing just one thing gets you started.

I learn to trust myself by taking action in small, everyday activities.

~ Day 115 ~

Is God trustworthy?

When I first knew God was real I needed to know if I could trust it. I experimented by turning over difficult situations, "I give this to you. Tell me what to do with it and that's what I'll do. I release the outcome to you." With each situation, I learned that the Beloved was wise, loving and trustworthy. Finally I turned my whole life over—a good decision!

> *As I experiment with the God of my understanding, I discover that it's trustworthy. I'm safe with my God.*

~ Day 116 ~

Sharing a friend's dream

When a friend shares a dream with me, I feel as if I've received a precious gift. The outer covering of the gift is the excitement that lights up their face and animates their words. The gift itself is the opportunity to tap into their joyous expectation, hold the dream on their behalf and then bear witness to their dream as it unfolds.

> *With joyous expectation, I hold my friend's dream on their behalf and then watch it unfold.*

～ DAY 117 ～

Dumping guilt

Making amends is a positive step toward freeing me from guilt. Guilt generates heavy negative energy in the world and doesn't help anyone. Every time one person dumps the guilt they've been carrying around, it lightens the load for all of us, creating a space for worldwide self-acceptance, self-worth and self-love. An open-hearted "I'm truly sorry" positively affects us all.

Making amends is good for me and good for the world.

～ DAY 118 ～

My attitude is creative

I'm the thinker of my own thoughts. The gloomy thoughts that run through my mind were created by me—the thought-maker! When I tell myself, "I can't do that," it's me, Jane, who has done the thinking. Since I'm the one who has created the thought, I'm the one who can challenge it. With new awareness I affirm, "I can do that!" My actions follow, and my life changes.

I'm a powerful creator! I affirm positive thoughts and follow up with positive actions.

~ Day 119 ~

Treating myself well through loss

Loss, including death, and the grief that comes from it, are normal and natural parts of living. Avoiding the pain doesn't make it go away—it only hides it for a while. Facing our loss allows us to accept and deal with it fully. When we treat ourselves well through our grief, we're much more apt to treat ourselves well after the pain subsides and we continue with our life.

I treat myself well through my grief and as I continue with my life.

~ Day 120 ~

Everything is sacred

The Creator created all-that-is out of itself. Therefore everything is holy—people, rivers, roads and buildings, frogs and ice cream cones. Reach out and touch something now and know that it's blessed. Touch your face, as you too, are a blessing. If God disappeared there would be nothing left, but instead here we all are, each of us part of the magnificence of the One that created us.

Everything is sacred—including me. We're all part of the magnificence of the One that created us.

~ Day 121 ~

Permission to be courageous

I give myself permission to be courageous. Even though I have a habit of letting my fears keep me from doing the things I want to do, I needn't continue doing so. Instead of that old "I'm afraid so I can't do it" mindset, I can prove to myself that courage is alive and awake within me. I take one tiny step at a time to say yes to the things I want to do. It's my life, my courage, my determination and my choice.

Courage is alive and well within me. I say yes to the things I want to do.

~ Day 122 ~

Honest communication

Those who are enthusiastic about what they're doing naturally want us to do the same thing. If it truly matches what we want, we can jump on board. If not, it's time to create a loving boundary instead of making excuses or avoiding them on that issue. Open, honest communication gives them the space to live their life fully, while we do the same with ours.

My open, honest communication creates the space for each of us to live our lives.

~ Day 123 ~

Rejuvenation or procrastination?

In our daily lives there are natural times of inactivity. How we view them is important—are they rejuvenation or procrastination? Rejuvenation is part of the creative process, allowing inspiration to emerge as we rest. Procrastination is full of *shoulds* and *shouldn'ts,* including "I shouldn't be resting right now." Accepting rest as part of the creative process allows for true rejuvenation.

> *As I accept rest as part of the creative process, it allows my creativity to flow.*

~ Day 124 ~

Within my sanctuary

I retreat into the sanctuary of my own divine self—the part of me that's unencumbered by outside circumstances. I become aware of my breath. My body relaxes, knowing it's going to take a break from the stresses of the day. Focused on the beauty and truth within me, I allow myself to just BE. My sanctuary awaits my attention. I turn toward it, rest in it, and I am renewed.

> *Within the sanctuary of my own self, I am renewed.*

~ Day 125 ~

When happiness is elusive

Happiness is often elusive. Things don't work out the way I wanted. I feel hurt, disappointed, my heart is broken. I honor my heart, feeling the ache . . . the brokenness. Then slowly the healing begins. God's will for us is to be happy. My heart knows this, and so do I. The sun will shine again . . . and so will I. The universe holds me as I let healing happen.

When happiness is elusive I honor the hurt in order to let the healing begin.

~ Day 126 ~

Great job!

When I'm very old I want to look back and say, "Great job! You're leaving the world in better shape than it was before you joined it!" Right now there's still time to leave my mark— each kindness to another matters, whether it's a friend, stranger, animal, plant, or our Mother Earth. Because I've learned lots about kindness in my lifetime, giving back is a joy!

At the end of my lifetime I'll look back and know I've left the world in better shape than it was before I joined it.

~ Day 127 ~

One kindness can change a life

One simple act of kindness can change an entire life. When my daughter started 8th grade in a new school, she felt very lost. Then a girl noticed her and said, "Hi! Do you want to hang out with us?" They're still good friends today, with kids of their own! We all want to be noticed and valued. We all matter. We all have worth. We're all Life's blessings to the world.

One act of kindness can change everything for both the giver and the receiver.

~ Day 128 ~

Choosing peace

One of the most powerful practices I've found is deciding to be peaceful when life feels chaotic. I know the chaos is temporary, and how I move through it is what's most important. If I focus on the chaos I'm inviting more drama into my life—yuk! If I focus on peace (aka the Beloved) I invite peace into the present moment, as well as peace in my future. It's worth doing the work to make it so.

When life feels chaotic, I can focus on the God of my understanding and invite peace into the moment.

~ DAY 129 ~

I can have a change of heart

When I stop criticizing myself, I tend to quit criticizing those around me. As I let go of negative self-talk, I'm more apt to speak kindly to others. As I release self-defeating thoughts, I make room for the daily changes in life. I begin to see through new eyes. My life rearranges itself around my change of heart, and the whole world is bright and new!

As I have a change of heart about myself, I see the world through new eyes.

~ DAY 130 ~

Nurturing my dreams

Isn't it remarkable that a mighty oak tree lies dormant within a tiny acorn? Once that acorn is nurtured with soil, water and air, it grows into the fulfillment of its grandeur! The infinite possibilities of blissful fulfillment lie dormant within us, too. When we nurture our dreams with belief, faith and action, we birth the light of Love within us, and a joy-filled life becomes our reality!

As I nurture my dreams, I birth the light of Love within me, and a joy-filled life becomes my reality!

~ DAY 131 ~

Simple joys

With appreciation, I let this day unfold, seeing what it holds for me. I notice the simple joys of showering, brushing my teeth and eating each meal. I tend to the business of the day in peace and harmony. I notice unexpected thoughts and feelings, paying attention to what they're telling me. Without the need to hurry through this day, I live it simply, fully and gratefully.

With appreciation, I notice and give thanks for life's simple joys.

~ DAY 132 ~

Taking ownership of my life

There's no getting around ownership of my life. When I give my life to someone else, playing small to please or appease them, I must eventually own the consequences of my actions. When I buy into someone else's fears and limitations, I have to own those consequences, too. On the day I start to choose personal happiness for myself, I am free.

As I take ownership of my life, personal happiness and freedom become my choice.

~ Day 133 ~

Creating the space for possibility

In our fast-paced world, it's easy to feel overwhelmed by life circumstances. Let that feeling of overwhelm be a gentle reminder to slow down, take a step back and breathe in a fresh, renewed feeling of faith. In any life circumstance, faith creates the space for unlimited possibilities to make themselves known. What we do with any situation is up to us. It's a joyous gift to allow faith to guide us to the highest good for everyone.

In any situation I bring the gift of my faith, creating a space for unlimited possibilities to make themselves known.

~ Day 134 ~

My story doesn't define me

The story of who I used to be no longer defines me. I'm not the same person I was when I was fifteen, young in experience and awareness. I'm not the same person I was when I was fifty, first realizing that God was real. I've learned such a lot since then — appreciating the process of learning, growing and changing. The person I am this moment is brand new.

My story doesn't define me. The person I am this moment is brand new.

~ Day 135 ~

Letting go of stress

When I go to bed fretting over a painful experience, I can almost guarantee that I'll wake up exhausted. Then stress permeates my day, causing me to see positive situations through negative eyes. Finally, when I feel so awful that it catches my attention, I ask myself why I'm hanging on to something I can give to the Beloved to hold. What a relief to free myself up to move forward!

I don't need to hang onto stress. Instead I give it to the God of my understanding.

~ Day 136 ~

Held in love

At the age of ninety-eight, my mom died. She was ready. As each development in the dying process unfolded, my prayer was one of surrender, "I give her to you, dear Beloved One, because you know the big picture for what's happening in this moment." My beautiful, atheist Mom was being held in the arms of grace. I held her as she passed, as the greatest Love of all held us both. Mom may not have believed in God, but it was abundantly clear that the Beloved believed in her.

My loved ones are held in the arms of the greatest Love of all as they die, as are those who cherish them.

~ Day 137 ~

Holding on

Have you ever been in a situation that felt totally out of your control and filled you with fear? The only thing you could do was hold on and keep reminding yourself that it will pass? Me, too! I look back on those times and realize the Beloved One was right there, giving me the strength, courage and endurance to hold on.

> *When life feels totally out of control, the God of my understanding is right there, giving me the strength, courage and endurance to hold on.*

~ Day 138 ~

Clarity in decisions

Making a decision, big or small, can be stressful. Memories of past experiences remind me of all the times I was wrong, bringing up emotions that leave me incapable of clear thinking. I ask myself, "What advice would I give someone else?" This helps remove the emotional snags that have nothing to do with the person I'm advising, which clears the cobwebs from my own mind. Clarity! I can now see what's best for me.

> *Asking, "What advice would I give someone else?" helps me gain clarity.*

~ Day 139 ~

Rebirth is a process

I've been reborn many times in my life—saying no to a dangerous situation as a teen, saying yes to falling in love the first time, going to college, leaving my marriage, taking care of my mom and then quietly rejoicing for her as she left this life. With every milestone, I shed part of the old me to embrace who I've become in that moment. Rebirth is a continual, sacred process.

Every milestone offers rebirth, as I shed the old to embrace the new me. .

~ Day 140 ~

My thoughts belong to me

No one has power over what I think. If I continually focus on someone else, it's my choice to do so. It also means that what they say and do determine my happiness as my own life passes me by. No one else is to blame for where I place my focus and what I'm thinking. If I want my life to be different, I'm the only one that can make that happen. My thoughts belong to me and today I choose them well.

My thoughts belong to me and today I choose them well.

~ DAY 141 ~

Big challenges

Big challenges ask us to own our greatness. We can dislike the situation, but it doesn't make it go away. As spiritual beings we're poised and ready to accept the challenge. As spiritual beings having a human experience, we can turn inward to the part of us that knows what to do, discovering a greater sense of the amazing clarity, wisdom, and creativity that resides within us, waiting to be activated.

When big challenges hit I turn to the part of me that knows what to do.

~ DAY 142 ~

My bedding

Soon after I knew God was real I had a new experience as I got into bed one night. The Beloved was the pillows, sheets, blankets and the bed itself! As I snuggled in, preparing to sleep, I was being lovingly embraced by the God that adores me in the form of my bedding! That feeling has never left—every night I nestle into the Beloved's embrace as I drift off to sleep.

As I nestle into bed at night, I'm held in the embrace of the God of my understanding.

~ Day 143 ~

Church has many faces

I'm grateful that there are so many religions and faith traditions. Each offers something for those of like mind. I'm grateful for nature, spiritual literature and music because they represent church for lots of people. It's all the same God . . . the same love . . . the same wisdom. The Infinite One is in all things, all the time. Each person's spiritual path is right for them and my path is right for me.

> *Knowing that church has many faces, my spiritual path is right for me.*

~ Day 144 ~

Making a difference

Because the energy of divine love is alive within us, it nudges us to reach out to make a difference in the world. Often we don't even realize we're making a difference! Just think of the times you intuitively said the right words when you thought you wouldn't know what to say, or you connected with someone only to find out how much they needed attention that day. We are love in form, and that's what love does.

> *Because I am love in form, I intuitively know what to say and do to make a difference in the world.*

~ DAY 145 ~

Re-evaluating my choices

As a child, I learned what to think and how to respond to different situations by following the examples of those around me. Whether the responses of my role models were empowering or defeating was not something I had the wisdom to figure out at the time. Without making anyone wrong, I can now re-evaluate the choices I make as an adult. We're all growing, doing the best we can with what we have.

I thoughtfully consider what I learned as a child in order to re-evaluate the choices I make today.

~ DAY 146 ~

My new normal is love

I used to hang on to victimization because it felt familiar; it's what I knew. Then the Beloved entered the picture. I quickly learned that I mattered in the world, with dreams to be realized and joy to be lived. Forgiveness became my new friend, teaching me to let go of victimization and say yes to the happiness in my heart. My new normal is love.

Remembering that I matter in the world, I forgive and say yes to happiness. My new normal is love.

~ DAY 147 ~

Uncovering the gifts in difficult times

When I think of the most difficult times of my life, I give thanks. First of all, I survived—I'm still here! My fears and doubts humbled me, teaching me empathy for those who are struggling today. My challenges taught me to absorb skills that seemed so easy for others, and yet I learned. I can look back with regret and resentment, or I can uncover the gifts and shine the light of gratitude. Gratitude wins!

Uncovering the gifts in the difficult times in my life, I choose gratitude for all that I've learned and who I've become.

~ DAY 148 ~

Making significant changes

Making significant changes brings with it the opportunity to know yourself at a deeper level. Decisions like beginning a new relationship, ending an old one, changing careers, or moving far away invite lots of life changes. You ask, "Is this right for me?" As you find yourself on the threshold of the old and the new, your inner wisdom stands ready to guide you to your highest happiness. You will know what to do.

As I contemplate making a significant change, I listen to my own inner wisdom and know what to do.

~ Day 149 ~

Listening and learning

In any dialog, if I insist that I'm right then I'm also insisting the other person is wrong. The middle way is to take our conflicting viewpoints in stride, offering an opportunity to expand my understanding of the many ways life can present itself. Genuinely listening to another's point of view doesn't mean I've changed my mind—what is does mean is that I've listened and learned.

Listening to another's point of view with an open mind helps me stay teachable.

~ Day 150 ~

As natural as turning on a light

Every conscious decision begins with a mental thought about it. When we walk into a dark room we make a mental decision to turn on a light. Gratefully, we can also make a mental decision to discover the spiritual light of our soul. In times of stress we can consciously decide to look toward our soul for guidance. With practice, it becomes as natural as turning on a light.

Looking toward my own inner wisdom is as natural as turning on a light.

~ DAY 151 ~

Furry, scaly and feathered friends

Sometimes our very best friends are furry, scaly or feathered. What a joy to have a pet that makes your heart smile when you think of them! Taking care of them becomes an extension of taking care of yourself—your pal's contentment becomes your delight. We were meant to give love and receive it. Our pets remind us that we are worthy of love in all ways.

My pet reminds me of how much I matter.

~ DAY 152 ~

Breaking the habit of pessimism

Pessimism is a habit that can be broken. These days I pay attention to the thoughts that run through my mind. When I catch myself being pessimistic, I challenge myself to look at it differently. As my focus changes, I quit using words like terrible, disgusting, and awful. I start using more words like fantastic, amazing and wonderful. Some habits are made to be broken!

As I challenge my old pessimistic habits, I make way for optimism and joy.

∼ Day 153 ∼

Giving my worries to my God

When things seem to fall apart I dive into the Beloved and ask, "What do I do with this?" Love whispers, "Breathe," which is my reminder to give up all control except my own positive response to the situation. If I've started taking on the beliefs or worries of another, I need to stop. My job is to steadfastly give all worries to the Beloved to handle. What a relief!

Remembering to breathe, I hold onto my positive thoughts and give my worries to my God.

∼ Day 154 ∼

Noticing the little delights

In the pursuit of happiness lots of people are looking for their dream. If this is you, start noticing the little delights in your life, like a hot shower, a deep breath of fresh air, laughing out loud, your car after its been washed, that first cup of coffee or watching your favorite movie again. Simple, everyday joys become a gateway to the dream that awaits your attention.

As I notice the little delights in my life, I'm paving the way to see the dream that awaits my attention.

~ Day 155 ~

Connecting the dots

Looking back at life's challenges is kind of like connecting the dots - suddenly it makes sense. I wasn't given those hard times for no reason—I grew through them! Did I know I was growing at the time? No way! I felt totally inadequate for the problems at hand, and yet somehow I found my way through them. Now I know I'm capable, courageous, tenacious and strong!

> *As I connect the dots of challenges, I see that I'm much more than I thought myself to be.*

~ Day 156 ~

Accepting kindness

I'm learning to be comfortable with receiving—letting someone do something kind for me, giving me a compliment or helping me. My part is to take it in, feel it deeply, and fully accept it because I'm worthy of receiving it. I needn't feel guilty or try to do or say something nice in return. My job is to simply say, "Thank you."

> *I let myself receive kindness, simply saying "Thank you."*

～ DAY 157 ～

Detaching from the problem

L ife challenges create fear and confusion. My first thoughts are, "This has to be fixed! I have to find a solution!" However, the chaos in my mind doesn't leave much room for clarity. Gratefully, my own inner wisdom stands ready to guide me. In prayer, I detach from the problem and relax into the awareness that a solution is at hand. My job is to listen, be patient and have the courage to follow divine direction when it's given.

Life challenges lead me to prayer, relaxing into the awareness that a solution is at hand.

～ DAY 158 ～

The vibration of optimism

B ecause we're made of God-stuff, we're ripe for creative expression. When we get into the rhythm of our true nature, the universe notices! If every day we're a little bit happier, a little more optimistic, our vibration attracts more happy and optimistic circumstances. Just imagine a world in which we're all vibrating with the expression of creative, joyous optimism! Opened wide to possibility, just think of the world we'd create!

Every day I'm a little happier, a little more optimistic, and soon the universe brings me more to be happy and optimistic about!

~ DAY 159 ~

Courage to follow God's will

God's will for us is complete happiness—that's it, plain and simple. It takes courage to follow God's will because I'm often sent in brand new directions. Where I used to think I was a wimp, I've discovered that I'm brave! I listen to divine direction and then act on it. There's a lot to learn as I step into brand new situations. As I'm busy learning, the universe does its part behind the scenes, and doors start to open on my behalf. It really is a co-creative dance, and when I let love lead, happiness shows up everywhere!

As I find the courage to follow God's will, happiness shows up everywhere!

~ DAY 160 ~

Shaking it off

Sometimes I see or hear something negative that gets stuck in my head, going round and round like a revolving door. Then I remember what happened after I used to give our dogs a bath. They would give themselves a mighty shake, fluffing their fur before getting on with the adventures of their day. I can do the same thing—shake it off! I needn't take my thoughts so seriously.

Remembering not to take my thoughts too seriously, I shake off the negative and get on with the adventures of the day.

~ DAY 161 ~

It's a process

Spiritually, we're very capable of loving everyone because we recognize their spiritual essence. Humanly, those closest to us often know how best to push our buttons, which causes us not to feel very loving. There's a balance here—while we're in the process of learning not to let our buttons get pushed, we needn't invite the button pusher home for a meal.

While I'm learning not to let my buttons get pushed, I needn't invite the button pusher home for a meal.

~ DAY 162 ~

Stories disguised as truth

In the past, I often told myself made-up stories about others that got me into trouble. Before I ever entered into a conversation I just knew it wasn't going to go well. I'd feed myself negative messages about them and stubbornly stuck with it as "truth," sabotaging the discussion before it had a chance. These days I do my best to quit telling myself made-up stories. I'm open to a greater truth, and life sure is easier!

No more made-up stories! Today I listen to a greater truth, and life is much easier.

~ DAY 163 ~

Misery and happiness are choices

Everyone wants to be happy, but choosing happiness is a different story. In each moment will I be as happy as possible or will I let the circumstance override my decision? Misery is a choice. Even if it's a miserable situation, can I find a small measure of peace and hope? Yes! Holding onto hope reminds me that things will get better, which helps me stay on the side of happiness.

> *Even in a miserable situation, I can find a measure of peace and hope. I choose to stay on the side of happiness.*

~ DAY 164 ~

I'm proud of myself because . . .

During the day there may be a dozen things I did well, but I focus on my mess-ups. Instead of self-worth, I'm filled with guilt and feelings of inadequacy. The only person doing this to me is me, and I'm the only one who can turn it around. Now each evening I look back on my day and finish the sentence, "Tonight I'm proud of myself because . . ." I'm owning my worth!

> *At least once a day I complete the statement "I'm proud of myself because . . ." I'm worth my time and attention!*

~ Day 165 ~

Stepping into my greatness

As you step into your greatness, those you love may become uncomfortable. Through caring or fear they may try to deter you. They will tell you why your decision/dream/next step makes no sense and won't work. My family's still scratching their heads about me becoming a minister! Your dream is bigger than anyone else's discomfort or fears. You're supported by a universe that's designed to help you succeed. It's your life—live it!

My dream belongs to me. I own it, I believe in it, and I'll live it!

~ Day 166 ~

Worthy and wise

I've made lots of mistakes. The Beloved meets them all with unconditional acceptance and love. I ask, "What do I do now?" Love answers, "Be kind to yourself. Instead of seeing what's wrong with you, see yourself as I see you—a beautiful reflection of me—worthy and wise, just as you are." We're all worthy and wise, even in the middle of our biggest mistakes.

Even in the middle of my biggest mistakes, I'm still worthy and wise.

～ Day 167 ～

Radiance of my creativity

The artwork you draw, paint or sculpt is one of a kind. Your book, poem, or spoken word carries a message unique to you. Your song embodies your melodic essence. Your garden becomes a delight of textures and colors brought to life under your care. The radiance of your imagination's creativity shines a light on a new possibility that had been waiting to happen through you.

The creativity of my imagination shines the light of a new possibility emerging through me.

～ Day 168 ～

Clearing away clutter

Clearing away physical clutter does a lot more than create a welcoming living or working space—it's an avenue to healing. The clutter got there because of some internal unrest. With conscious intention, clearing away a tiny portion of the clutter every day can create a new mindset that soothes those old fears with reassurance that it's safe to let go of what's no longer needed. What was true yesterday no longer needs to be true today. Freedom leads the way.

One tiny bit at a time, I soothe old fears by letting go of what's no longer needed.

~ Day 169 ~

A brand new life!

Officially being in the 'senior' category is glorious! It gives me time to go after the things that are important to me now that I've had a lifetime of experience and learning to work with. I never would have considered myself an author, but now I've got a lot to write about. I wouldn't have considered myself an artist, but now I paint constantly! Being a senior is an invitation to jump right into a brand new life!

Being a senior is my invitation to do what's important to me now.

~ Day 170 ~

Experiences come and go

Life is such a variety of experiences—we just never know what's going to come our way. A huge range of emotional responses ensue. Sometimes there's a jolt of panic and sometimes a delight that puts a smile on our face. No matter what emotion shows up, it doesn't last. It comes for a while, we feel it, and then it's gone. There's no need to hang onto it. Learning from each experience and then letting it go creates the space to live fully in the moment now.

Every experience comes and goes. As I let go, I make room to learn from the experience I'm having right now.

~ Day 171 ~

Saying yes to me is okay

Evidence of old beliefs lay thick in the collective consciousness of the human race. The saying *It's better to give than to receive* hints that we should always put others before us, that saying yes to ourselves isn't okay. There's a new love-consciousness rising! When we love and honor ourselves we bring the fullness of our unique energy to the world. Saying yes to ourselves is quite okay!

Saying yes to me is okay. Putting me first is okay. Feeling good about me brings my positive energy to the world.

~ Day 172 ~

Reminders

The Beloved seeks to find ways for us to notice its presence. The satisfaction of our morning coffee, hearing our favorite song, a call from a friend, or the glow of the moon is not happenstance—this is love's way of saying, "Here is my gift to you. Know that I see you. I know you. I love you. You are my cherished one."

The Beloved's gifts are reminders that I am precious to God.

～ DAY 173 ～

Problem or opportunity?

My perception of a situation is either defeating or empowering. If I see it as a problem I label myself a victim, full of anxiety and doubt. I start looking for threats and unhappy endings. If I see it as an opportunity to grow I tap into the part of me where strength, wisdom, inspiration and new options live. Opportunities help me become the person I want to be.

What look like problems are opportunities for me to grow into the person I want to be.

～ DAY 174 ～

Setting healthy boundaries

Knowing what you want is one thing. Doing something about it is another. Once I knew God was real I finally learned to set healthy boundaries—speaking up and taking appropriate action where necessary. It took courage! In the process I realized that healthy boundaries equal self-respect and self-worth, which in turn equals a healthy life.

As I set healthy boundaries, I create a healthy life.

~ DAY 175 ~

Going easy on myself

When I have deadlines to meet, errands to run, and my to-do list is overflowing, my sense of calm can go right out the window. It's tempting to blame myself with self-defeating "I should haves." My life works a lot better when calm is restored. I stop, take a breath and slow down. Then I make a commitment to go easy on myself. Whatever I do today, I will let it be enough.

I take a breath and slow down. Whatever I do today, I will let it be enough.

~ DAY 176 ~

Vibration of truth

Detecting my soul's silent message, I sense the vibration of truth. I feel the resonance of my response, tears overflowing with the emotion of it all. The dance begins as I say yes, becoming willing to follow. In the sacred holiness of the dance I surrender, willing to be led by the part of me that wants only my highest good. The result is sweet and strong and sure. It changes me.

I lean into the message of my soul. Becoming willing to follow its divine direction, I am changed.

∼ Day 177 ∼

Smiling as a healing force

We generally equate smiling with happiness, and it can also initiate healing. Smiling can be a powerful remedy for the sadness that comes when we continually concentrate on our problems. We can make a personal commitment to raise our spirits by shifting our focus from what's bothering us to the positive energy of smiling at loved ones, co-workers, pets, friends and strangers. It's amazing how the connection we make with others can diminish the effects of our problems. Smiling opens the floodgates of healing to the situation!

Instead of focusing on my problems, I make a conscious decision to smile at everyone, bringing the positive energy of healing to the situation.

∼ Day 178 ∼

Opening my eyes

When I want to feel the Presence, I just open my eyes and look around. There is not one thing that is not God in form. I touch my clothes or the chair I'm sitting on and thank them for being in service to me. I thank the sun for showering me with its warmth and the trees for their shade. The God that adores me exists in all things, all the time.

The God that adores me exists in all things, all the time.

~ Day 179 ~

Everything has purpose

Remember that relationship, business venture or project that didn't work out? All isn't lost. There was something in it for you—it had meaning and purpose. You may not know what it is now, but at some point you'll know. Perhaps it added to your staying power, your flexibility, or your ability to let go. We live in a friendly universe. Nothing in your life goes to waste.

> *Everything in my life has meaning and purpose. Nothing goes to waste.*

~ Day 180 ~

Letting go of resentment

Letting go of even the tiniest bit of resentment creates space for a whole lot of joy and inner peace. Joy and inner peace are who we are as spiritual beings. Resentment is a human thing. It clogs the wheel of the joy and inner peace that are meant to flow throughout every human experience. Letting go of one little bit of resentment at a time allows the goodness of life to start flowing again.

> *Every time I release even a tiny bit of resentment, I make room for joy and inner peace.*

~ DAY 181 ~

What if I won the lottery?

Seeing things from a new perspective is helpful. What if, in the middle of a really difficult situation, I found out I had just won the lottery? Would my mood change? Might it alter the way I handle the situation? When I'm swept up in negative emotions over any challenge, I'll ask how I'd feel if I just won the lottery. Why not embrace that new perspective with its corresponding positivity right now?

> *By asking, "Would I still be this upset if I knew I had just won the lottery?" I gauge my perspective and embrace positivity.*

~ DAY 182 ~

Fun!

I pulled into my garage but didn't turn my car off before the song on the radio was over. Why? Because I was singing out loud, dancing to the music! Life doesn't need to be so serious, and we weren't created to be inhibited. Sure, sometimes we need to act like adults, but we're also supposed to have fun! There are so many simple pleasures, and we're meant to enjoy them!

> *Whenever possible, I take the opportunity to thoroughly enjoy life's simple pleasures.*

~ DAY 183 ~

My body tells me the truth

If you listen to your body it will tell you the truth. It will tell you if you're settling for less than you're worth or let you know that you're trying to keep your real feelings hidden so that you don't rock the boat. It will help you know if you're living the life you were born to live or if you're trying to pacify those around you. You'll know if you're letting your light shine or finding ways to dim it. Once you awaken to the truth your body conveys to you, the healing of your life is at hand.

My body tells me the truth. Today I listen to its message and take action, knowing that healing is at hand.

~ DAY 184 ~

Spiritual beings

As spiritual beings we've chosen to have a human experience. Our lifetime will contain doubt and confidence, resistance and acceptance, guilt and forgiveness. We'll learn what it's like to be humbled, to feel joy, and to know fear. Within each situation the reality of absolute peace and grace are available, for they are at the core of our being.

As a spiritual being having a human experience, I remember that peace and grace are at the core of my being.

~ DAY 185 ~

Break out!

By nature we're restless . . . an inner urging to break out and try something brand new! When we stifle that urge, opting to stick with the status quo, we feel unfulfilled and end up taking it out on ourselves or others. Sometimes we get sick. Often we act out with behavior that's not in our best interest. At the very least we feel crabby. Instead of holding back, wouldn't it be easier to hold onto faith, break out of the doldrums and go for what excites us?

When I have an inner urge to break out and try something new, I go for it!

~ DAY 186 ~

I am precious

You are precious to the God that adores you. It's not just because it lives through you, as you— it's because the Beloved is over-the-top in love with you! Whether you're having a good day or a terrible day, you are Love's cherished one. What if you went to sleep tonight repeating, *"I am precious to the One that adores me,"* and really believed it?

I am precious to the One that adores me.

~ Day 187 ~

My mind is a creative machine

The universe pays attention to what I'm thinking. When I declare, "I don't want this negativity in my life!" I'm focusing on the very negativity I don't want, which brings more negativity into my life. My mind is a creative machine! It's time to monitor my thinking, choose optimism, and find reasons to be grateful. In focusing on the positive, the negative begins to fade away.

When I find myself focusing on the negative, I turn my life around by replacing it with positivity.

~ Day 188 ~

Following a big dream

Do you have a dream that's so big your mind can't contain it? Following that dream may make no logical sense, but your heart knows what it's doing. Your dream calls for a willingness to be led in a wider direction, a walk into the unknown with a faith that overrides uncertainty. We were made for expansion, to live a larger truth, to love our lives more deeply, and to create the reality that's true for us.

Sensing a big dream that's mine alone, I walk into the unknown to bring it to fruition.

~ DAY 189 ~

Smiling is good for me!

Research has shown that smiling when I don't feel like it is good for me! My body and my brain team up to make me feel better. The physical facial movements of smiling tell my brain to lighten up and see the world more optimistically. Smiling kick-starts the positivity process! Now when I'm feeling cranky I walk around with a smile on my face, and you know what? It works!

Smiling is good for me! I walk around with a smile on my face because I deserve to be happy.

~ DAY 190 ~

Checking my attitude

The energy of our attitude determines the kind of experiences we'll have. When jealousy and suspicion make our lives miserable, we'll end up in more situations where the same energy thrives. It's a reminder to check our attitude! As we re-focus on gratitude and self-worth, jealousy and suspicion fall away, replaced by the inner peace born from our new attitude.

If my life isn't as happy as I want it to be, I'll check my attitude and make needed adjustments.

~ Day 191 ~

Self-care

The beginning of anything is generally filled with expectation, excitement, angst, and lots of other intense emotions. The ending may encompass relief, joy, regret, or other equally powerful feelings. The middle is where the learning happens, where we grow the most. It's our opportunity to treat ourselves with respect, letting self-awareness be tempered with gentle self-care.

During the learning process I treat myself gently.

~ Day 192 ~

Breathing together as one

In the quiet I become sensitive to the aliveness of all life's creation, breathing together as one. In the stillness, I sense the synchronistic energy of love in form and that which is without form. My body awakens and my heart stirs. I catch the rhythm of life's breathing and in unison I breathe with her. With gratitude, I know without a doubt that we are all one.

In the quiet I breathe with the rhythm of life itself, knowing that I am one with all of life's creation.

~ Day 193 ~

Noticing the small gifts

There are times when my life seems askew. I need something, but I can't pinpoint what it is. Because the Beloved knows me intimately, it cares about the smallest, silliest things that I might be overlooking. As I pray to know that as my daily needs are met, my heart is opened to notice and appreciate every gift that shows up, knowing it will be so.

> *When my life seems askew, I pray to notice and appreciate*
> *every tiny gift that shows up throughout my day.*

~ Day 194 ~

Letting others do it their way

Remember when you were a child and got into trouble for doing something your way instead of the way you were told? When you got older there was the boss who reprimanded you for handling a situation your way instead of how it had always been done? Recalling those feelings help when I'm tempted to tell someone how they should live their life. No matter what it looks like, we each have the right to do it our way.

> *As I live my life in my own way, I give others the right to*
> *do the same.*

～ Day 195 ～

Expecting doors to open

It's safe to expect doors to open for you. Your job is to let go of how it will happen and what the result will be. You are worthwhile just as you are, no matter what your life looks like or what horrible things you've done. The universe is making the way possible on your behalf because it thinks you're magnificent! So get on with your day and enjoy it, secure in knowing that your good is in process.

> *Knowing that the universe thinks I'm magnificent and my good is in process, I enjoy every minute of my day!*

～ Day 196 ～

Acknowledging powerlessness

In Al-Anon I heard that I was powerless over other people. Really? I thought it was my job to make them happy! Of course, when they didn't follow my suggestions I felt like a victim, and in my victimization I became powerless. I learned that the only person I had power over was me. My new focus resulted in letting go of victimization. As I took my power back, freedom reigned!

> *Acknowledging powerlessness is a first step toward freedom.*

~ DAY 197 ~

Good is growing in the world

The goodness of life shows up all around me! When I see an adult enjoying a child or a pet owner delighting in their pet, my heart stirs. When I notice a young person offering a helping hand to another, I know that good is growing in the world. These days I see it more and more—we're learning to reach out and connect, treasuring each other in the simple joys of life.

As I notice our connections with each other, I know that good is growing in the world.

~ DAY 198 ~

Choosing a good mood

If I start my day by consciously choosing a good mood, it will help me stay the course when I'm tempted to complain, make someone else wrong, defend my actions, or play small in any way—my job is to like myself in each situation! My good mood reminds me to treat myself gently when I goof, knowing that I'm worthy of a second chance. My mood sets me up to enjoy my day fully!

I start my day by choosing a good mood, which enables me to like myself in each situation.

~ Day 199 ~

Prayer for moving through challenges

Oh Divine Infinite One ~

I surrender my journey through this challenge to you. I give you my frightened, hopeless self to make way for the courageous, faith-filled self that I know exists within me. Taking responsibility for my life, and knowing I'm never alone, I choose to walk through this difficulty with confidence and grace. For this I am grateful. Amen.

I move through this challenge with confidence and grace.

~ Day 200 ~

Taking a break

Have you ever been inspired while you're in the shower? Me, too! In the moments of pure relaxation, the flow of creativity is high. In the middle of going about my day, I often sense that it's time to take a break. As I go get the mail, take a walk, make a meal or put in a load of laundry, a brand new idea surfaces! Taking a break is a wonderful way to get back in the flow.

Taking a break helps me get back into the flow of life.

~ Day 201 ~

Loosening drama's hold

The drama around me can be intoxicating—my very own soap opera! When I buy into it I jump into darkness. My thoughts become judgmental, my outlook pessimistic, and my attitude cynical. My answer is to take life's drama in stride, noticing it without buying into it. Using my magnificent, creative will power, I make a conscious decision to move out of the darkness and into the light.

I take life's drama in stride. I may notice drama, but I no longer buy into it.

~ Day 202 ~

Taking care of me

Taking care of me, valuing me just as I am, takes practice. Just like any new behavior, it takes diligence and repeated repetition to let go of old beliefs, to say yes to what I want, no to what I don't want, and to forgive myself when I fall back on old behaviors. Taking care of me may seem very unnatural at first, but when I stick with it I realize that I'm worth my own self-understanding, self-respect and self-care.

I take care of me! I'm worth my own self-understanding, self-respect and self-care.

~ DAY 203 ~

Let your light shine!

You may have been raised to take care of everyone else first, putting yourself on the back burner. Today's a new day! You were meant to shine the light that is you! When you stand in the glory of your own authentic self, you want to share—your service to others comes from the absolute joy of giving! It not only illumines your light, it sets an example for others to do the same. We're all meant to shine, sharing the gift that is us!

I stand in the joy of my own authentic self and share the gift that is me!

~ DAY 204 ~

God-gifts in nature

The abundance of the universe shows up in miraculous ways! Deep in the forest the early morning fog settles in, bringing a blessing to all that thirsts during the dry season. Fog droplets condense on the needles and leaves of trees, dripping to the ground where they can be absorbed, just as if it had rained. Noticing God-gifts in nature helps me see them in my own life.

When I notice the God-gifts in nature, I start to see them in my own life.

~ Day 205 ~

Respectfully honest communication

I feel most comfortable with people who are respectfully direct . . . candid . . . honest. I know where I stand with them. They speak their mind and say what they want. If there has been a misunderstanding, they will ask me about it. What a relief! No more walking on eggshells, guessing what another is thinking. Today I choose to be around those who value open communication.

I surround myself with people who value respectfully open, honest, direct communication

~ Day 206 ~

Saying yes to me

When I will no longer be treated badly by another, I'm saying yes to me. There's a reason a sense of disquiet has been building up within me. It's a God set-up, reminding me that my life can be so much more than what I'm accepting for myself. It's time to speak up, own my courage and live my worth. Change is at hand. Thank you, dear life, for nudging me forward.

Today I speak up, own my courage and live my worth. I say yes to me!

~ Day 207 ~

Shake things up!

On one of those days when life feels boring and nonproductive, shake things up! Try doing one new thing. Make it big! Find someplace to volunteer and commit to it by actually signing up, take a different route from work and stop to take pictures of what you see, eat with someone you've never shared a meal with before, sleep outside, take a midnight stroll and laugh at the moon. You'll feel better!

> On a blah day I'll shake things up by doing something big and new. I'll feel better!

~ Day 208 ~

I'm gutsy, smart and strong!

In the past I often saw myself as weak in difficult times—not strong or wise enough to succeed at what I really wanted. Oh, the stories I could tell about failing! Today I give myself permission to change my perspective. I start looking for all the ways I've succeeded. I tell myself new stories of facing the storms and moving through them. I'm gutsy, smart and strong!

> I give myself permission to change my perspective. I'm gutsy, smart and strong!

~ DAY 209 ~

Walking through fear changes me

Every time I walk through fear, my light shines a little brighter. I trust myself more. I discover what it feels like to have faith in my intuition . . . my gut instinct. My body feels the difference between the stress of fear and the power of "doing it anyway." I stand a little taller on the other side of fear, aware that I am changed.

As I walk through fear I learn to trust myself. I stand taller, aware that I am changed.

~ DAY 210 ~

One thing at a time

Choosing to be peaceful has caused me to slow down. Whenever possible, I let go of multi-tasking. Instead of doing two or three things, I do one thing mindfully. I peacefully approach each next task. Honoring myself, I pay attention to one feeling at a time. I notice and appreciate one pleasurable experience at a time. Releasing a sense of urgency creates peace in my life.

Choosing to slow down creates peace in my life.

~ Day 211 ~

Continuity of life

As a spiritual being, I am eternal. I'm aware that at some point, my physical body will die. As I become free of my physical body, I will experience the spaciousness of infinity, of which I'm a part. I'll be held in the embrace of the Infinite One as I reacquaint myself with eternity, rejoicing in the limitless choices from which to incarnate. Choosing, I'll step into form once again as the continuity of life continues.

> *As a spiritual being, I'm eternal. Letting go of my physical body, the continuity of life continues.*

~ Day 212 ~

Letting myself be seen

There were times when I built a protective wall around an old pain so that I could get on with my life. Eventually that wall kept me from being the person I wanted to be. The authentic me couldn't show up because the hurt me was hiding behind that wall. Finally, I became secure enough in myself to let the wall crumble. What a relief to show up and be seen!

> *As I let my protective wall crumble, I stand tall to show up and be seen.*

~ DAY 213 ~

Embracing change

Everything changes all the time, and yet we seem to struggle with moving forward. We tend to look back to past disappointments, and hesitation sets in. In reality we're set up to succeed — the creative intelligence of the universe is the stuff from which we're made. It's time to raise our expectations, embrace change and step into our greatness!

Knowing that I'm made of the creative intelligence of the universe, I embrace change and step into my greatness!

~ DAY 214 ~

What I allow will continue

What I allow will continue. If I allow myself or others to speak to me in a disrespectful way, it will continue. If I allow myself or others to take me for granted, it will continue. The good news is that once I'm aware, it can all change. When I quit allowing negativity into my life, I automatically invite positivity in. I'm the one who can set a new boundary, and I'm the one who's worth it!

As I release negativity, I make room for positivity in my life.

~ DAY 215 ~

Picking myself up to start again

Just think of how capable you are! When a challenge occurs it may stop you for a while, but not for long—if that was true you'd still be sitting on the road after falling off your first bike! Make a list of all the times you've picked yourself up and started again, including every change that was difficult. Realize that you can feel safe within yourself. You really do know what you're doing.

> I've picked myself up and started again many times! I really do know what I'm doing.

~ DAY 216 ~

Stronger and wiser

Past painful circumstances can either keep me from enjoying today or help me grow stronger. When I'm so afraid of being hurt again, I'm tied to the initial pain and it becomes my identity. When I let my past pain team up with the healing power of courage and faith, I become stronger because I know something new about navigating life—I'm now wiser. With the strength and wisdom born from experience, I pick myself up and one tiny step at a time, I move on.

> With the strength and wisdom born from experience, I move on.

~ Day 217 ~

The messiness of moving forward

Moving forward can get messy. Birth is messy, too, but worth it. Being open and honest can be messy and also very freeing. Messiness is part of the journey. It's taught me not to take myself too seriously and to have compassion when my life or another's life is messy. Messes are the Beloved's reminder that creation is in process. It's time to treat ourselves gently.

Within the messes of moving forward, I treat myself and others gently.

~ Day 218 ~

Insanity

In Al-Anon I learned that the definition of insanity is doing the same thing over and over, expecting different results. No wonder my life was such a mess—I was insane! For years I'd tried to right the sinking ship of my life by doing the same things over and over. Finally, shaken to the core, I discovered my Higher Power. I then righted the course of my life by changing my focus, my attitude and my actions. Sure enough, my life started changing!

Letting go of insanity, I change my focus, my attitude and my actions. My life is brand new!

~ Day 219 ~

Small things count

One Sunday morning I was sitting at a red light with my family when I spotted a tiny kitten in the middle of the intersection. I jumped out of the car and scooped up the kitten. Then I noticed a church on the corner, and there stood the pastor. Handing him the kitten, I told him I had a hunch that someone in his congregation would want this tiny baby. Smiling, he agreed! Small things count in big ways.

Everywhere I go, in everything I do, I remember that small things count in big ways.

~ Day 220 ~

Love and compassion begin with me

Love and compassion feed both the giver and the receiver. The whole world benefits! Every single instance of loving compassion makes a difference, like a drop into an empty glass waiting to be filled. It begins with us—when we're compassionate and loving toward ourselves, we're seeing our light instead of our darkness. Then it's easier to see the light in others. One drop at a time . . .

When I'm loving and compassionate with myself, I can be loving and compassionate with others. The whole world benefits!

~ Day 221 ~

When disagreements occur

If a disagreement comes up and I know I need to talk to the person about it, I'm cautious about the need to have things my way. Disagreements can broaden my outlook about the world, moving me past my own limited perspective. Within any disagreement lies the potential for a brand new solution, one neither person has considered. My job is to be lovingly open to it.

In any disagreement lies the potential for a brand new solution. I stay open to it.

~ Day 222 ~

Without pretenses

Friends are safe with each other, no need for pretenses. With loving-kindness, each has found a special nook inside their heart where the other abides, free to be themselves with all of their special, outrageous, beloved kookiness. With openhearted caring, friends allow each other to just BE.

My friends are free to be exactly who they are—me, too!

~ DAY 223 ~

Saying no is empowering

I've learned the power of saying no to the people and situations which are not in my best interests at the time. Saying no has created time to slow down, be quiet and listen to the whisperings of my soul. Saying no loosens me from the sometimes frantic energy of the world. I don't need to acquire the latest technological device or jump onto the next committee. Instead I say yes to silence, simplicity, creativity and community. It feels good!

I say no to what isn't right for me so I can say yes to what is right for me.

~ DAY 224 ~

Change agents

Sudden and unexpected challenges are change agents. They force me to become stronger, wiser, and more courageous. The alternative is to cave into the problem. Change is often messy as I learn and stumble and grow, but I do grow, coming out the other side a different person. My greatest difficulties have helped uncover the depth and the strength of the person I am.

Challenges help uncover the depth and strength of the person I am.

~ Day 225 ~

Watering my dream-seed

You may have a dream that others around you can't see. Watching you take a chance frightens them, so they try to pull you back. Don't let it stop you! Keep watering the dream-seed that's alive in your heart. The universe will help you grow it. You have nothing to prove to anyone except yourself, and that's everything.

I water the dream-seed that's alive in my heart, knowing the universe will help me grow it.

~ Day 226 ~

It's not my job to fix others

It's freeing to know it's not my job to fix others. Everyone has within them the wisdom and grace of a God that adores them. When and if they're ready to change their life, their soul stands prepared to guide them. If they choose to change, it's their journey, not mine. If they don't choose to change, it's still their journey, not mine. My job is to accept them, just as they are.

It's not my job to fix others. My job is to I accept them, just as they are.

~ Day 227 ~

Surrendering to my own evolution

A sense of sacred isolation is often part of a spiritual journey. Whereas religious paths are generally well-traveled by the group, your true calling may beckon you into unchartered territory where no path exists. On your own, you follow divine direction. Your faith grows as your own path emerges. Surrendering to your own evolution, you discover the glory of your own worth.

Surrendering to the beauty of my own evolution, I willingly follow the path before me.

~ Day 228 ~

Standing for what's important

The changes that are part of my daily life offer the opportunity to stand for what's important to me. I say faith is important, but is that what I stand for in the situation, or do I jump into fear? I want peace to come first, but do I cave into the drama around me? The universe loves me so much that it notices where I put my attention and gives me more of that. If I want to change my life I can use each moment to consciously stand for what's important to me.

In each moment, I consciously create the life I want by standing for what's important to me.

~ Day 229 ~

Feel like a kid again!

How long has it been since you've participated in a childhood favorite? Try it! Slide down a slide, throw a ball, blow bubbles, swing on a swing, tell a knock-knock joke, watch cartoons, read a favorite children's book, eat your favorite childhood snack, sing childhood songs, walk in puddles, or finger paint! Let yourself feel like a kid again!

Life is meant to be enjoyed! Today I do something fun to feel like a kid again!

~ Day 230 ~

I matter in the world

Every life experience matters. Each has led to who I am today. Positive experiences have awakened a sense of joy, creativity, gratitude and love. Painful experiences have taught me endurance, courage, and the willingness to change where necessary. With each experience I've gained a depth of self-awareness that shines a light on the beauty that I am today. Just as I am, I matter in the world.

Each life experience has led me to who I am today. Just as I am, I matter in the world.

~ Day 231 ~

Vibration of my choice

If I want more money and have prayed for prosperity, and then I find a dime, I'm at creative choice. I can be dissatisfied because it's only a dime or thrilled because it's evidence of answered prayer. The universe pays attention to the vibration of my choice. If I'm excited I invite prosperity into my life. My disappointment shuts the door on prosperity. Everything matters!

My prosperity grows as I celebrate every bit of answered prayer.

~ Day 232 ~

Healing my tender places

When I'm open to healing, I can be pretty sure that an emotional trigger is going to come my way as an opportunity to heal that sensitive place within me. Making a conscious decision to practice being strong within my tender place, I build my emotional muscles. My emotional muscles tell me I no longer need to carry my hurt around as I move through my day. With the focus on healing instead of being hurt by the trigger, I grow my inner strength.

With my focus on healing, I can use triggers to grow my inner strength.

~ Day 233 ~

Letting go of victimization

It's easy to feel victimized in just about any situation, even the good things—buying a new car can be a joy or it can be a constant worry about making the payments. Thinking of family can fill me with gratitude or remind me of our problems. Donning the victim hat can easily become habitual. Learning to take it off reminds me to take responsibility for where I put my focus. Today I refuse to think, speak or act like a victim.

Taking responsibility for my life, I refuse to think, speak or act like a victim.

~ Day 234 ~

Self-kindness in mistakes

My thoughts are noticed by the creative universe. When I think of myself kindly, especially when I've goofed big-time, the universe pays attention to my self-kindness, not my goof. Today I choose self-kindness. I embrace the moment of my messiness and optimistically make the most of it, setting into motion a kind and optimistic tomorrow.

When I've made a big goof I choose self-kindness, setting into motion a kind and optimistic tomorrow.

~ Day 235 ~

Challenging old beliefs

One of the most courageous things I can do is challenge what I always believed to be true. Lots of my beliefs are those I grew up with. Some are still relevant today, but many aren't. What I believed in the past isn't the truth anymore unless I keep it alive in my mind. Challenging the old invites shiny new beliefs to become real in my life today.

I gather my courage to challenge old beliefs that no longer serve me.

~ Day 236 ~

My life inspires me

I'm inspired by the world's greatest thinkers, the deeds of those who have made significant changes in people's lives, and the insight of saints of every religion. That inspiration remains just a series of good ideas unless my own life inspires me. Can I be kind when someone disagrees with me? Can I be proud of how I move through daily activities? Today, may my own life inspire me.

As I become the best me I can be, I am inspired by my life.

~ Day 237 ~

Trusting myself

The Beloved reminds me, "Don't hold on too tight. Let your life ebb and flow, discovering the gifts in each moment. Move through life without clinging. Freedom comes with faith, and faith comes with knowing the beauty of who you are in each situation . . . in every life circumstance. You were created to be happy. Let me prove it to you. Trust that you will know what to say and do as you go along. Your beauty shines when you do your best and then let go of the outcome."

Freedom is mine when I move with the ebb and flow of life, trusting myself in each situation.

~ Day 238 ~

The urge to de-clutter

The sudden urge to de-clutter is a God-thing. One day I awakened at 3:00 a.m. with the desire to clean out a particular closet, so that's what I did. It was the Beloved's nudge, letting me know it's time let go of the old and clear a path for a new thought, idea, awareness or action—whatever God has in mind for me. Sometimes accepting the invitation for transformation is as simple as cleaning out a closet.

In acting on an unexpected urge to de-clutter, I accept the invitation for transformation.

~ DAY 239 ~

Making way for healing

When we've lost someone dear to us, including our pets, it's important to take time to process our grief. It doesn't mean that we're becoming mired in sadness—it means that we're honoring our loss. There's no time-limit to the grieving process—it takes as long as it takes. Allowing ourselves to be fully in the process makes way for the self-care of healing.

Being fully in the process of grief makes way for self-care as I heal.

~ DAY 240 ~

The Beloved's precious ones

There's a lot I don't know about the Beloved. How can it possibly know all of its creation so intimately all at the same time? How can it understand what's in our minds and hearts before we understand it ourselves? How can it love each of us as if we were the only one in the world? I no longer try to figure it out—instead I accept it as true. We're all the Beloved's precious ones, just as we are.

It's true—I'm the Beloved's precious one, just as I am!

~ Day 241 ~

Releasing my grumpiness

If my life seems a bit unbalanced with grumpy people, it's an opportunity to look at any grumpiness within myself. The vibration of my happiness or my discontent draws to me others who are happy or discontented. Who do I want to hang out with? First I have to *be* it! As I release my own grumpiness, my happiness will invite others who are happy—much better!

As I release my own grumpiness, my happiness invites other happy people into my life.

~ Day 242 ~

Keeping promises

When I make a promise to another, I do my very best to keep that promise. It feels good to be a person of my word. When I make a promise to myself, it's even more important that I keep it. It reminds me that I am worthy of keeping my own promises. With each promise kept, I prove to myself that I can treat myself well with my own best behavior.

The most important promises I keep are the ones I make to myself.

~ DAY 243 ~

Sharing my gifts

When I'm at peace, the energy of my peace flows out into the world in ways I can't see but I know are real. Every time I pray, someone I've never met will feel it and be comforted. Every moment of peace, every prayer stretches across the universe to be felt by another. We are powerful creators! When we treat ourselves well, we offer the same gift to the world.

When I treat myself well, I offer the same gift to the world.

~ DAY 244 ~

A gift to myself

Forgiveness is perhaps the greatest gift we can give ourselves. Honoring ourselves, we relish the promise of this moment instead of pulling guilt and blame from the past into it. Today I choose to live my life fully, seeing what's before me with fresh eyes, open to the creative power of NOW. God's will for us is to be happy, and today I accept it!

I give myself the gift of forgiveness in order to live my life fully today.

~ Day 245 ~

Warmed by the light of Love

When I'm feeling unsure, my soul s directs me to turn toward the light of the sun. Just as the sun's rays make their way into the darkness of the tiniest crevices, the light of my truth finds its way into the hiding spots within my mind . . . the spots where my insecurities hide. Gently, the warmth of my own light encourages my insecurities to come out of hiding, to be warmed by the light of wisdom, clarity and love.

When I'm unsure, my insecurities are warmed by my own light of wisdom, clarity and love.

~ Day 246 ~

Momentum of enthusiasm

Usually a good night's sleep is important. I've also realized that when I'm in the middle of a writing project, my enthusiasm carries me through. I wake up very early, brimming with ideas, and fly down to the computer to get going! I tell myself, "I'll sleep later!" as I begin my day with a giant grin on my face.

The momentum of enthusiasm creates a great day!

~ Day 247 ~

Courage to begin again

Just like you, I've stumbled and fallen more times than I can count. I've doubted that I had what it takes to get back up and start again. But I did it! So did you! When we had no idea what to do, somehow we found what we needed, pulled ourselves together, and started again. We're more than we think we are. We're strong. We're smart. We're courageous. We can begin again!

I'm strong. I'm smart. I'm courageous. I can begin again!

~ Day 248 ~

When pain seems insurmountable

Sometimes the pain of life seems insurmountable. It's hard to be calm enough to listen for the still, small voice within, assuring me that I'm going to be okay. In actuality, my inner wisdom is already speaking to me, encouraging me to feel my feelings, even though it hurts. My pain is birthing something resilient, courageous and amazing in me. Later I'll look back and know that it's true.

When life feels so hard, I'll lean into it, knowing that something resilient, courageous and amazing is being birthed in me.

~ DAY 249 ~

I'm positively amazing!

If you're determined to feel better about yourself, your determination becomes the foundation upon which your life will transform. It's time to believe in the new you! Try tucking a note into your pocket, or tape it in your car or your mirror that says, 'You are amazing—absolutely, positively amazing!' Pledge to smile every time you see it and you'll soon start to believe it!

I am amazing—absolutely, positively amazing!

~ DAY 250 ~

My joy matters

We're meant to live our lives, not just let time pass. We're meant to discover what excites us and then do that. The energy that comes from our joy makes its way into the vibration of the universe, uplifting people we've never met but now somehow feel better about life. The spark of our joy becomes the spark of their joy, and so it goes. Our joy matters!

As I do the things that excite me, the energy of my joy uplifts others.

~ Day 251 ~

Receiving life's abundance

Life is always trying to give from its abundance—my job has been learning to allow myself to receive it. The more I deepen my faith, the more fulfilled my life becomes. As I listen to divine wisdom instead of the limited thinking in my mind, more miracles show up. Leaning into love not only feels good, it allows me to receive from its bounty.

As I deepen my faith, I gratefully receive from the abundance of life's bounty.

~ Day 252 ~

Crying as prayer

Crying is a really effective form of prayer. When tears start to flow, I can feel my defensive walls crumbling, which lets divine love in. I needn't say a word, as the Beloved already knows what my tears are about. Resting in the comfort of the greatest Love of all, the longer I cry the better, as every tear shed is part of my sacred prayer. There's a reason I feel lots better after a good cry.

My tears are a prayer. I let them flow.

~ Day 253 ~

I can create a glorious life!

With my powerful mind I can create a glorious life! Knowing how divinely loved I am leads to a feeling of self-worth that's deep, true and enduring. I'm meant to be happy, simply because I exist. With my accepting heart I take action, stepping out into the unknown. I allow myself to accept the fantastic life I'm meant to have.

With my powerful mind and my accepting heart, I take action, accepting the fantastic life I'm meant to have!

~ Day 254 ~

Taking the high road

I'm always at choice as to how to view a situation. Humanly, a knee-jerk reaction is tempting, but that leads to a perception that's narrow and very one-sided (my need to be right). When I take the high road I see from a larger perspective . . . a wider angle . . . an expanded viewpoint. From the high road I can see my part in it without the need to own the outcome.

As I take the high road in any situation, I can see my part in it without the need to own the outcome.

~ Day 255 ~

My scary places

We needn't try to hide our fear, our anger, our self-blame or anything else from the Beloved, for it already knows us better than we know ourselves, including all our human feelings. It meets us at the center of our biggest worries, our greatest fears and in those dark days when life feels like a cesspool of muck. When our scary places are touched by pure love, transformation takes place.

I trust the God of my understanding with my scary places, allowing transformation to take place.

~ Day 256 ~

Curiosity stretches me

Curiosity stretches me, "What would it be like to take a class, try a new recipe, investigate that store you keep wondering about or take a leisurely walk around the local lake?" When I make the decision to satisfy my curiosity, I re-discover the joys of being fully present in the moment. While I work toward my long-term goals, I needn't forget the delights available to me right now.

Curiosity helps me enjoy the delights available to me in the moment.

~ Day 257 ~

Solitude

Solitude is high on my priority list. Being away from distractions helps clear my mind and relax my body. I move into a receptive state, *being* instead of *doing*. From the wisdom deep within me, solutions to problems surface and next steps present themselves. Then creativity starts to flow. New ideas seem to come out of nowhere! I live in a friendly, abundant universe. Solitude offers me access to it.

Moments of solitude help me receive the creative goodness of the universe.

~ Day 258 ~

Accepting success

At my first book signing I had an underlying feeling of embarrassment. What's that about? Here I was, living my dream, and my ego was shouting, "Who do you think you are?" Clearly, I wasn't used to the spotlight and the praise that goes with it. Gratefully, I concentrated on signing the books so I wouldn't goof. By the end of the book signing I was mostly done with feeling small. Accepting success really can be a process, can't it?

Accepting success gives me the opportunity to say yes to who I am today.

~ Day 259 ~

Changing the sheets

It's pure heaven to crawl into bed after changing the sheets—clean, smooth, no wrinkles. By morning the bed's all wrinkly, kind of like life. I can start off with the best of intentions—clean and smooth—but wrinkles develop because they're a natural part of life. So I practice holding a positive attitude and things begin to smooth out, just like changing the sheets!

When wrinkles develop throughout the day, I practice holding a positive attitude to smooth them out.

~ Day 260 ~

Gratitude for all of it

These days I pay attention to what I think and say about my life. When I look back I'm grateful for all of it—every single experience. No longer do I wear the sad, droopy victim hat. Today I put on my imaginary happy-hat because I like who I am. Gratitude for my past is part of liking who I am today. When a challenge comes along, I intend to look back on it with gratitude, too.

I'm grateful for every life experience—each has helped me like who I am today.

~ Day 261 ~

The maverick in me

Once you decide to own your life, you'll discover the maverick in you. No longer will you let others do your thinking or speak for you. Instead you'll have a new respect for your own ideas because you'll have a new respect for yourself. From deep within, you sense a greater wisdom from which the maverick is born. As you follow its divine guidance, you move out from the crowd to pave your own way.

The maverick in me helps me move out from the crowd to pave my own way.

~ Day 262 ~

Boundaries = self-respect

When I finally became aware of my lack of boundaries, I understood that it was due to a lack self-respect. I wanted others to like me more than I felt I deserved to like myself. When I gently started to release old beliefs, I made room for self-worth. Setting boundaries based on my growing self-esteem, I was embraced with the knowing that I am precious to life, just as I am.

I set boundaries because I respect myself, knowing I am precious to life.

~ DAY 263 ~

When fears come true

Most of my fears have come true—a loved one died, the job was lost, the relationship ended, the money went away. Although each was really hard and sometimes the struggle lasted a long time, I survived. Solutions surfaced. Courage made itself known. Inner strength was fostered. Healing happened. The God of my understanding not only helped me get through each challenge, it helped me come out stronger on the other side.

When fears come true, I'll come out stronger on the other side.

~ DAY 264 ~

When apologies don't happen

I may never get the apology I seek. Focusing on anger and resentment carries my bitterness from the past into today, attracting more situations in which to feel victimized because apologies aren't offered. I am not my history! In my mind and heart, I can hear and accept the apology I never got. I can then put the experience behind me and step fully into today, creating the joy-filled future I deserve.

As I put my past behind me, I create the joy-filled future I deserve.

~ DAY 265 ~

Below the surface

Flowers bloom, wheat fields flourish and trees grow into their magnificence from the essential combination of sun, dirt and rain. What we see is the result of what's taken place below ground. We can appreciate someone else's life, knowing there's been a lot of dirt and rain below the surface that we see. Holding ourselves gently, we realize the same is true for us.

The beauty of who I am comes from the dirt and rain below the surface.

~ DAY 266 ~

My God is stronger than my problems

Before I knew God was real I hoped for a life free of struggles, but they came anyway. In the middle of the mess I wished my problems would go away. On the other side of my problems I was relieved that they were gone and then started worrying that troubles would find me again. An endless cycle! Today the cycle is broken. I've quit worrying. My God is much stronger than my problems.

When I'm tempted to worry I remember that my God is much stronger than my problems.

~ Day 267 ~

Learning from my inner light

When my self-esteem is low I let others take advantage of me, which perpetuates my feelings of unworthiness. Hopelessness sets in. All the while there is a light within me that refuses to be dimmed. It keeps shining until I finally see it. That light is a great self-worth teacher. I am already enough! Little by little my self-esteem grows until I stand tall in the light that I am.

I am already enough! I stand tall in the light that I am.

~ Day 268 ~

Drama crossroads

I've discovered that drama doesn't just appear by itself. I've somehow created it, invited it into my life, or associated with others who create or invite it into their lives. This brings me to a crossroads—if I want drama in my life I can keep doing what I'm doing. If not, I can give myself permission to change my own behavior and when necessary, walk away from the drama created or invited by others.

I'm done with drama! I quit creating it in my own life and walk away from it in others' lives.

~ Day 269 ~

Getting out of a slump

I can find lots of reasons/excuses to stay in a slump when my mind is mired in slump thinking. Un-slumping myself must become more important than the alternative of staying slumped. My heart sings out, "Get going! You're not too tired, too old or too wounded to start." Listening to the encouragement of my own inner cheerleader, I let the un-slumping begin!

Choosing to get out of a slump, I listen to the encouragement of my own inner cheerleader and let the un-slumping begin!

~ Day 270 ~

We're all blessings

To the Beloved everyone is cherished, no matter what faith tradition we follow, if any. We're all beautiful souls created from the same Source, unique in our own thoughts and beliefs. Whether we call ourselves Christian, Buddhist, Jewish, Muslim, Hindu, atheist or agnostic; whether we practice Native American, New Thought, or pagan traditions, or no traditions at all, we're blessings in love's eyes.

No matter what I believe, I'm a blessing the eyes of divine love.

~ DAY 271 ~

Magic of imagination

We're all born with the magic of imagination—creativity, silliness and joy embedded into our spiritual DNA. In childhood, our imagination has a field day! Everything is possible! As we grow up society cautions us to stop being so silly. We're told to act our age and be responsible. In the process some of that magic starts to fade. The good thing is that we've never really lost it. It's still there, ready to be reactivated. Let the fun begin!

Today I reactivate the magic of my imagination. Let the fun begin!

~ DAY 272 ~

No more guilt!

I used to be an elementary school teacher. As summer vacation approached, I felt guilty for not teaching summer school—heaven forbid I'd just rest! In order to compensate, I'd create a major project for the summer. It took years to realize that I'd earned this time of rest, that it was okay to lay around, take naps, watch TV and read novels. Today I know better. In knowing better, I treat myself better.

Today I allow myself times of rest—no guilt allowed!

~ Day 273 ~

When loved ones hurt each other

Sometimes those I love hurt each other. I set a boundary for myself, knowing it's not my place to interfere. Instead I give them to the Beloved for safekeeping. I picture the energy of divine love around each of my loved ones—they are held in love's peace and grace. This allows me to get on with living my life, as it's the only life I can control.

> *When those I love hurt each other, I give them to my God for safekeeping, remembering that my life is the only life I can control.*

~ Day 274 ~

I am worthy, I am loved

I live in a universe that was created to support me, supplying my every need and much more. If that's not happening, it could be that I'm hesitating to believe that I'm worthy and deserving of Life's bounty. If this is the case, I sit in the silence and repeat, *'I am worthy, I am loved'* at least one hundred times twice a day. As my consciousness shifts, so does the quality of my life.

> *I am worthy, I am loved.*

~ Day 275 ~

Hurtful words

When I'm the recipient of someone's hurtful words, it's generally not about me. It's likely they're redirecting anger they've been holding onto without being aware of it. I may remind them of someone they haven't forgiven, a past hurtful experience, or they may be angry at themselves and are taking it out on me. Detaching from their words, I do my best to meet them with kindness, remembering that I too have been less than gracious when I've been angry.

Knowing that someone's hurtful words aren't about me, I do my best to meet them with kindness.

~ Day 276 ~

I'm not broken

When my life is a mess the Beloved simply allows it to be. Because there's no judgment with divine love, there's no need to fix me because there's nothing wrong with me—I'm not broken. I was given free will and a powerfully creative mind for a reason—it's up to me to head my life in a new direction. When I lean into love for guidance, I know which path to take.

I'm not broken. I lean into divine love for guidance and head in a new direction.

~ DAY 277 ~

Living consciously in each moment

Because I know that the death of my physical body is a certainty, my intention is to live life fully now. That doesn't mean I need to be accomplish great feats every day—instead it means that I consciously live each moment. If I want to spend hours curled up with tea and a good book, I relish in the experience! When the time comes that my death is imminent, I want to look back at my life and know that I have lived.

Knowing that one day my physical body will die, I live my life fully today.

~ DAY 278 ~

Restrooms as prayer rooms

Restrooms are perfect for prayer! If I find myself in an uncomfortable position at work, home, at a party, or just about anywhere else, I quietly excuse myself to use the restroom. First good thing: no one's going to question my request. Second good thing: I can close the door, shut my eyes, get centered and pray. Third good thing: I emerge renewed and refreshed, knowing what to do next.

When I need to take a break, collect my thoughts and say a prayer, restrooms become a haven.

~ Day 279 ~

Making a difference

A lot of learning goes into a lifetime, not just schoolbook learning or learning on the job, but the learning that comes from being alive in the world, interacting with life on a daily basis. As we get older, we have a chance to put all that learning to work to make a difference in someone else's life right now. So we help a neighbor, become a volunteer, send a card or offer a smile. It all makes a difference.

Right now I can make a difference in someone else's life.

~ Day 280 ~

From victim to believer

Faith becomes a way of life when I let it. Choosing faith in difficult circumstances changes the way I see it, transforming me from a victim to a believer who knows that somehow good will come from the situation. Because my thoughts are powerful creators, my faith not only changes the way I deal with the challenge, it also changes the outcome.

Choosing faith transforms me from victim to a believer who knows that good will come from the situation.

~ Day 281 ~

Button-pushers

I used to get my buttons pushed to the point of pure frustration, taking it very personally. Sometimes I noticed that when the button-pusher would do the same thing with someone else, that person wasn't even fazed by it. Finally I realized that it was my *reaction* to the button-pusher's words and actions that was making my life miserable. I found a new inner strength in non-reaction.

> *I choose non-reaction instead of allowing my buttons to be pushed.*

~ Day 282 ~

Going with the flow

When I allow myself to be in the flow of life, good things happen seemingly out of nowhere! Life is so much easier! When I insist on having my own way, I dam up the flow of life and wonder why everything's a struggle. The universe naturally flows in the direction of my happiness because joy, abundance and creativity are its nature. That's my nature, too! No wonder going with the flow works so well!

> *As I go with the flow of life, I'm going with the flow of my own nature. Good things happen!*

~ Day 283 ~

Staying true to myself

Along the way, many well-meaning friends and family members have tried to talk me into doing something that they're doing because it's working so well for them. Surely it will be equally as wonderful for me! The trouble is I don't want to do it. When I've caved into their urgings I've been sorry. When I've stayed true to myself by saying, "No thanks," I'm right on target!

When I stay true to myself, I'm right on target!

~ Day 284 ~

Creating peace

Choosing to be peaceful has caused me to slow down. Whenever possible, I let go of multi-tasking. Instead of doing two or three things, I do one thing mindfully. I peacefully approach each next task. Honoring myself, I pay attention to one feeling at a time. I notice and appreciate one pleasurable experience at a time. Releasing a sense of urgency creates peace in my life.

Slowing down, mindfully doing one thing at a time, creates peace in my life.

~ DAY 285 ~

Seeing in a new way

I think I know something because my mind tells me it's true. After that anything unlike that truth becomes false. The idea of a friendly universe that wanted me to succeed was nonsense to me. Finally, I hung around spiritual folks and listened to my own intuition long enough to become willing to change my mind . . . to see it a new way. My new truth opened up a whole new world for me!

When I become willing to see something in a new way, a whole new world opens up for me!

~ DAY 286 ~

Releasing clutter

When I let go of physical clutter, I have breathing space. Freeing up time removes cluttering activities on my calendar that I don't really want to do, leaving blank spaces when I can relax. Letting go of emotional clutter releases people, situations and events that are no longer in my best interests. Releasing physical, time and emotional clutter brings about a space where the goodness of life can thrive.

As I let go of clutter in my life, I make space for the happiness I deserve.

~ DAY 287 ~

Channel for soul wisdom

You have within you a vast reservoir of creative potential. You know you've tapped into it when a new idea comes out of nowhere and you think, "Where did *that* come from?" Pay attention! The wisdom of your soul is seeking to make itself known through you. If you're willing to be a channel for divine inspiration, you'll be amazed at what happens!

I'm willing to be a channel for the divine inspiration of my soul.

~ DAY 288 ~

Being my own hero

We all have it within us to be our own hero. We were born with the courage, strength and power of the One that created us. Even if somewhere along the way we forgot who we are, it doesn't change a thing—the Creator's courage, strength and power shines within us. We already know how to move through every challenge. Our job is to pay attention, remember and act on it.

In every challenge I have what it takes to be my own hero.

~ Day 289 ~

Beginning concept of a Higher Power

When I first started Al-Anon as an atheist, I couldn't even imagine such a thing as a Higher Power. Instead, the group said I could use them as a beginning concept of a Higher Power, relying on their wisdom as I struggled with my insecurities and my faith. A fine idea! The rooms of recovery reflected the Beloved's unconditional acceptance of me just as I was.

My Higher Power comes in all forms, including people.

~ Day 290 ~

When friends grow apart

Over the years, friends may grow in different directions. They no longer have the same interests or priorities. Giving each other breathing space offers an opportunity to lovingly evaluate whether the friendship is one that is still in their best interests. If it is, they adjust and come together with a fresh perspective. If not, they release each other with love. Letting go can be a beautiful act of caring. All is well.

If my friend and I have grown in different directions, we can adjust or release each other with love. All is well.

~ Day 291 ~

Good for me!

It's give-myself-a-compliment day! I ask, "What have I done right today?" Did I brush my teeth for two minutes? Take out the garbage before it got stinky? Anything goes! Then I think back to five years ago—what's different about me today? How have I grown? What challenges have I made it through? Good for me! It's time to chalk up some well-earned compliments!

I happily look for reasons to give myself a compliment, and then I do it!

~ Day 292 ~

The energy of my enthusiasm is creative

After submitting my first book to eleven publishers and receiving a few rejects, I could feel my energy waning. I gave myself permission to stop for a while and do what I loved—write! A week later I woke up thinking, 'This is the day!" I submitted it to two more publishers. Both of them accepted it, and then a third said yes! The energy of our enthusiasm is creative. It's okay to give ourselves a break before starting again.

When my enthusiasm wanes I can give myself a break before starting again.

~ DAY 293 ~

God-speak

I'm awakening to the way the God of my understanding speaks to me. God-speak drifts through my open window as a soft breeze, connecting the outside with the inside. It awakens me from my night's sleep with a sense of newness for the day. God-speak is the feel of the floor under my bare feet and the running water on my hands as I rinse the dishes. In all things, at all times, God speaks to me.

In all things, at all times, the God of my understanding speaks to me.

~ DAY 294 ~

In the middle of the mess

There's something to be said for looking back at hard, really messy times to find the blessings contained within them. An unexpected blessing is remembering what it felt like to be in the middle of the mess, especially when I was at least partially responsible for it. It cultivates empathy and understanding for others who are in the middle of their own messes, knowing I've been there, too.

Remembering my own messes cultivates compassion for those who are in the middle of theirs.

~ DAY 295 ~

I choose to thrive!

Life is meant to be lived, not just managed. My calendar used to be packed with people and events! I thought this meant I was thriving . . . I was important . . . I was doing good things in the world. When I trimmed my calendar back to only what I truly *wanted* to do, I discovered what thriving really means! It leaves space to enjoy the parts of my life that are most important to me.

By making space to truly enjoy my life, I discover what thriving really means.

~ DAY 296 ~

My peace spills out into the world

As I let go of the need to fix others, I choose peace for myself. Peace has no agenda—instead it's a place of compassion and acceptance. Within peace I can accept differences without making one wrong and another right. When I live in peace, the energy of my acceptance flows through me and spills over, infiltrating every nook and cranny of the world.

As I let go of the need to fix others, the energy of my peace spills out into the world.

~ DAY 297 ~

In-between times

Life is filled with in-between times—the space in between what used to be and what's coming. Jobs and finances change, family stuff plays itself out, relationships shift, health issues arise, addictions are addressed, dreams are explored. We live in a generous, creative universe. We're meant to be happy. Holding onto faith during in-between times offers fertile soil for the very best outcomes.

During in-between times, my faith creates fertile soil for the very best outcome.

~ DAY 298 ~

I refuse to be a victim

I refuse to be a victim—that's old behavior. When I start sliding back into victimization it feels awful, so it catches my attention. Every potential victim situation is an opportunity to remember that I'm a lot stronger and wiser than I believe myself to be. I'm worthy of living a beautiful life! Calming my racing heart, I let go of victimization, choose a new thought, and get on with the life I deserve.

As I let go of victimization, I choose a new thought and get on with the beautiful life I deserve.

~ Day 299 ~

Take a time out

Occasionally grumpiness creeps up on me. Feeling tired and easily frustrated are indications that crankiness is at hand, a clear signal that a bit of self-love is in order. It's time to treat myself gently, take a time out, quit trying to do it all, and just stop for a while. Self-care is a sure-fire way to honor me just as I am, allowing that crabbiness to quietly fade away.

When I'm tired or frustrated I take a time-out—a bit of self-care is in order.

~ Day 300 ~

Learning empowers me

I got married when I was 21 and divorced when I was 51. Leaving my marriage was scary! Most frightening was learning all the things I didn't know how to do. But I did it! I learned, I made mistakes, and I learned some more. Every single time I did anything new (even if it wasn't right), I was empowered.

Every time I learn something new, I am empowered.

~ DAY 301 ~

Changing an old belief

Changing an old belief takes practice. It keeps showing up—I bump up against it over and over. It's kind of like telling a puppy she can't come into the kitchen. The rule is repeated, followed by action as the puppy is removed from the kitchen once again. As my old belief is repeatedly told it's no longer in effect, my new actions prove it to be so.

I practice changing an old belief in intention, thought, word, and action.

~ DAY 302 ~

Learning to ignore

Learning to ignore negativity can be a marvelous path to inner peace. By ignoring another's negative behavior, I'm not getting pulled into undesirable energy. When I ignore a hurtful remark, I'm not taking it personally. Choosing to ignore the fear-based mind chatter in my head, I get on with living my amazing life. A lot of good can come from ignoring that which doesn't belong in my life!

Inner peace is mine when I ignore the negativity that doesn't belong in my life.

~ DAY 303 ~

Forgiveness is my choice

When a conflict or disagreement occurs, even though the other person caused it or played a role, my feelings about it are my responsibility. I ask, "Do I want to stay angry or find peace?" I turn inward to forgive any part I may have played in the conflict—the thoughts, words and actions that didn't reveal my own spiritual nature. Then I do the same for the other person, forgiving the thoughts, words and actions that didn't reveal their spiritual nature. Forgiveness and peace are my choices.

My feelings about any conflict are my responsibility. Forgiveness and peace are my choices.

~ DAY 304 ~

Evaluating a relationship

Because change is normal, there are times when it's necessary to evaluate a relationship. Is it still having a positive effect on me, or am I spending precious time with someone who is no longer a match? It doesn't make the other person wrong—it just lets me know that it may be time for me to move on. Letting go with love, I embrace relationships that make my heart happy today.

I embrace relationships that make my heart happy.

~ Day 305 ~

Creating an expansive flow of time

When I remember the energy of my mind's own creative thinking, I can create an expansive, relaxed flow of time. I've experimented with it! If I'm in a time crunch and remember to say, "I have all the time I need," and really believe it, I find myself taking a deep breath, slowing down and relaxing. Very soon I start to hit green lights, slower cars move into another lane, I find the perfect parking space and arrive in plenty of time!

I create an expansive, relaxed flow of time by taking a deep breath and saying, "I have all the time I need."

~ Day 306 ~

Dumping my worry stories

I've found that my worries are really only interesting to me. No one else wants to hear the worry stories that roll around in my head, and they especially don't want to be sucked into them. What if my worries are only real in my mind? Nearly every time I've challenged my worries and gotten on the other side of them, they've evaporated. I'm going to quit talking about them and move through them instead!

I'm done with my old worry stories—I'm dumping them!

~ DAY 307 ~

Letting my dreams lead me

My problems used to get a lot of my time and attention. Then the Beloved came along and planted some beautiful dreams in my heart. *Really? Me?* Those dreams were so magnificent that my attention was now going in a brand new direction. I've discovered that when I'm led by my dreams, many of my problems start to take care of themselves. Most definitely a God thing . . .

> *When I'm led by my dreams, my problems take care of themselves.*

~ DAY 308 ~

Seeds of prosperity

Every so often I am delighted to find a coin lying on the ground, just waiting for me to notice it. As I pick it up my thoughts turn to gratitude and I whisper, "Thank you, gracious and abundant universe, for reminding me that this coin plants a seed of prosperity in the very fertile soil of my mind." Aware that my thoughts are creative, I'm grateful for the abundance that's making its way to me.

> *Gratitude for coins found on the ground plants seeds of prosperity in my very fertile mind.*

~ DAY 309 ~

Getting my life back on course

When the unexpected happens it's easy to feel turned upside down with no way to right the ship called 'My Life.' Gratitude is one way to create a path whereby my life gets back on course, headed in the right direction. I don't have to figure out how it will happen, but by looking for things to be grateful for in the middle of the upset, the universe automatically begins setting a course for the very best outcome.

When my life is off course, gratitude heads it back in the right direction.

~ DAY 310 ~

Easily pleased

People laugh at me because I'm so easily pleased. I don't have a lot of "favorites" since I'm mostly content with what's in front of me. I like all kinds of weather. I'm tickled about small things like laughing out loud and organic veggies. I don't get mired in debating whether someone or something is right or wrong—I'd rather lean into my own inner wisdom for answers. Being easily pleased is kind of like looking through love's rose-colored glasses.

As I look through divine love's rose-colored glasses, I'm delighted by the smallest things!

~ Day 311 ~

Message of my soul

Have you ever been talking to someone and all of a sudden you knew to be quiet, say nothing, and just listen? Listening to the message of my soul is kind of like that. It silences mind chatter and bypasses my need to hear my own opinion. In a flash nothing becomes more important than its message. In the silence I relax into what it is I'm supposed to know, and then I hear it.

In the silence I hear the message of my soul.

~ Day 312 ~

Growing past my perceptions

Seeds emerge as small plants when they break through their shell and reach for the sun, growing past the soil that has nurtured them. When flowers are ready they open to the light. In nature, growth is normal and natural. The same is true for us. We're intended to stretch past who we perceive ourselves to be to grow into the glory of who we truly are.

I stretch past who I perceive myself to be, growing into the glory of who I truly am.

～ Day 313 ～

Music is eternal

Have you ever wondered what happens to a musical note once you no longer hear it? I believe that its energy travels on to become part of the next song, touching the life of others who hear it. It's never done. Music is eternal. It lives forever, just as we live forever. In this lifetime I'm having a human experience. Perhaps in the next I'll be a musical note, having a musical experience.

Music forever touches the lives of those who hear it.

～ Day 314 ～

When remembering mistakes is helpful

There are times when it's helpful to remember my mistakes. My own embarrassing blunders can act as beginning points for empathy and compassion for others who have just made a major goof. Identification with how it feels helps me let go of my knee-jerk judgment. With a bit of understanding my heart opens, allowing just the right words to come out of my mouth.

As I remember my own mistakes, I have empathy for others who have just goofed.

~ DAY 315 ~

Hope is my life raft

Hope bubbles up from deep within me when I feel like I'm floundering. Hope is the life raft I crawl into to rest awhile, secure in knowing that I'm not alone, that I'm being held by the One who loves me unconditionally and knows I can thrive. So I float in my life raft of hope until my strength and courage return. Then I emerge, ready to begin again.

When my life is floundering, hope is my life raft.

~ DAY 316 ~

No limitations

Imagine yourself with no limitations—free to do and be whatever you want. What do you see? Where are you? What are you doing? Are there others around you? How do you feel? Stay with that vision and let it expand—it may be larger than your imagination can hold. It's the Infinite One's vision for your life, speaking to your limitless potential. The vision is meant for you.

Imagining myself with no limitations, I sense the vision for my life.

~ DAY 317 ~

Self-care in confrontational conversations

There have been times when I've excused myself and walked away from an inappropriate, confrontational conversation. Good for me for not getting sucked into it! There have also been times when I've been able to detach my emotional reactions from such a conversation without the need to walk away. Knowing that I have choices is empowering.

I'm at choice as to how to handle confrontational conversations. What's important is taking care of me.

~ DAY 318 ~

Seeing my greatness

I'm meant to have an amazing life! The universe stands ready to give me everything I want, plus more. Because I co-create with the universe, I play an important part. If I'm settling for less than I deserve, it's time to stop. If I've been identifying with my struggles instead of my potential, I need to stop that, too. When I see my greatness, the universe will know what to do with it.

I co-create my amazing life with a universe that supports me.

~ Day 319 ~

Balancing self-sufficiency

To be self-sufficient is rewarding—learning to take care of my own needs. To become overly confident in my self-sufficiency can lead to an undercurrent of fear. What happens if I can't do it, if I don't know all the answers, if I need help? My inner wisdom knows the path to the balance in all things, including the willingness to ask for help when needed.

My life is balanced with the confidence of self-sufficiency and the willingness to ask for help when needed.

~ Day 320 ~

Giving my full attention

I strive to really hear others. Giving my full attention to the person in front of me is among life's greatest gifts, and I want to do it well. Letting go of the temptation to multi-task, I choose a moment of true connection. Listening, I pause before immediately replying, giving me time to fully receive what the person has said. It's amazing how much I can learn when I truly listen!

I give my full attention to the person in front of me.

~ DAY 321 ~

My internal reminder

You may not think you have a personal relationship with the God of your understanding, but you do. It's your internal reminder to rest when you're tired instead of pushing yourself to do more, to treat yourself gently when your human imperfections surface, and to notice and be glad for life's small successes. Relax into love's connection—it's wherever you are.

The God of my understanding is my internal reminder to treat myself well.

~ DAY 322 ~

Animal connection

Animals remind me of my connection with all of life. We really are much alike! Our furry, scaled and feathered friends have different personalities, just like us. While some are more introverted, content with the quieter side of life, others stand out in a crowd, saying what's on their mind or singing to their heart's content! Each of us are being our very beautiful, authentic, glorious selves!

I'm grateful to notice my connection with all of life, including animals.

~ DAY 323 ~

My part of the mess

In Al-Anon I was invited to look at my part in the messiness of my life—yikes! I so wanted it to be someone else's fault! But avoiding the root cause of my pain kept me dancing around the process of healing instead of stepping into it. It took courage to look honestly at my own attitudes and behaviors to see how I had contributed to my problems. Learning to love myself through it, my healing began.

With loving acceptance, I take responsibility for my part in the messiness of my life.

~ DAY 324 ~

When I hurt another

It can be upsetting when someone snaps at us, seemingly out of nowhere, because there has been no hurtful intention on our part. We may have inadvertently pushed one of their buttons without being aware of it. No matter how well we think we know another, there are tender places within them that may be hiding in the shadows, waiting to be triggered. Without the need to understand what's behind their response, we can remember not to take it personally and open our heart to compassion.

When I inadvertently hurt another, I remember that I don't need to understand in order to be compassionate.

~ DAY 325 ~

Help me

Some of my most powerful prayers have been very short, "Help me," or "I need you." Sometimes they're long—I just keep rambling until I feel the Beloved's presence, and then a sense of relief fills me. No matter how I pray, what's most important is knowing I'm heard. In fact, the One that hears me knew my prayer before I ever started. I really am never alone.

No matter how I pray, I know I'm heard.

~ DAY 326 ~

Everything is energy

Knowing that everything is energy sure changes the way I look at life. Each situation has its own vibration, and I want to bring my highest energetic vibration to it. I pay attention to how I feel in that particular circumstance, noticing my body's response and staying alert to the messages sent by my intuition. Everything is alive and we're all part it. We all make a difference.

I bring my highest energetic vibration to each situation, knowing it makes a difference.

~ Day 327 ~

Joy!

The joy I feel in my heart can have an amazing effect on every aspect of my life. My body responds to joy with new energy—a sense of fun emerges! My interactions with others are rejuvenated. My work is infused with uplifting creativity. Unexpected prosperity shows up! My joy begins with me. The universe mirrors it back to me as the richness of my life.

I say yes to what makes me happy. The joy I feel infuses every part of my life!

~ Day 328 ~

Teachers offer the way

Teachers are all around us, helping us move forward on our spiritual path. They tell us that our power is within us. They see our potential when we can't see it for ourselves. By their example, we sense what's possible. Our teachers set before us a promising path to our own transformation, but it can only become a reality when we take the first step.

As teachers offer a way forward on my spiritual path, I become willing to take the first step.

~ DAY 329 ~

My mind holds my intentions

Because we humans are an emotional lot, it's easy to feel like we're losing something whenever change rolls around, which is often! The good news is that we can train our very powerful and creative mind to help us turn around our feelings of loss. With every change we can say to ourselves, "A blessing is going to come from this!" As our mind holds this intention, our positive new outlook opens the door to life's many blessings.

I use my powerful and creative mind to hold the intention "A blessing is going to come from this!"

~ DAY 330 ~

Shedding the old

Pets can teach us a lot. Anyone who's had a furry pet knows about finding fur on their clothes. Dogs and cats shed, birds molt and snakes loosen their old skin. The result? New fur, feathers and skin have room to grow. It's a reminder that letting go of the old makes way for something better. Giving thanks for the way we used to be, it may be time for us to do a bit of shedding so the very best can show up!

Giving thanks for the way I used to be, I now shed the old to make room for the very best!

~ Day 331 ~

Clarity

I've become clearer about life as I've gotten older. I'm able to stand up for what's important to me because I'm more aware of what truly matters. It's easier to stop trying to control others after finally realizing it's none of my business. I joyfully dive into the ways I can make a difference in the world, knowing that I can't do it all, but I can do my part. My newfound clarity is a relief for which I'm grateful.

As I get older, I'm clearer about what's important.

~ Day 332 ~

I choose my reaction

Other people's behavior belongs to them. My behavior belongs to me. When I'm in a circumstance in which my buttons could be pushed, I'm at choice. Without my reaction the incident has no power over me, and I'm in charge of my reaction. Ultimately it's not the situation that's important, but who I am in it.

I choose my reaction to any situation, knowing who I am in it is more important than the situation itself.

~ Day 333 ~

Stepping onto a new path

Life rarely goes as planned. Rather than questioning why things are the way they are, I do my best to accept them as is—this is my new reality. There's a brand new path in front of me. Summoning courage, I take the first shaky step. With each subsequent step my footing becomes more solid. More courageous than ever, I gratefully dive into the new adventure that is my life.

Accepting things as they are, I courageously step into the new adventure that is my life.

~ Day 334 ~

Our connection is forever

I am an eternal being. My soul . . . my God essence . . . my inner wisdom, has lived since the beginning of creation and will exist forever. Because this is true for all of us, when someone I love dies they are only gone in the physical sense. In reality, they are gloriously alive! They are in the sunrise, the air I breathe and the joy of laughter. Staying open, I sense their presence. As two eternal souls, our connection is forever.

I sense the presence of my loved one in the sunrise and the air I breath. Our connection is forever.

~ DAY 335 ~

Waiting

Waiting is a necessary part of success. I can take all the needed steps to bring a dream to fruition, and then I wait as the universe sets divine right action into motion on my behalf. While I wait, I often gain abilities that will be needed once my dream has manifested. Sometimes my dream even takes a different course! It's all important. Nothing is lost while I wait.

Part of bringing my dream into manifestation is waiting, knowing that waiting is a necessary part of success.

~ DAY 336 ~

Giving myself a chance

I've often hung on from fear. What will happen if I let go? Will it be worse than it is now? Because letting go invites the unknown to become a reality, it can be scary! Staying stuck tends to become miserable for a reason—so we'll let go. Now letting go is lots easier. It has grown my in myself. The result? My life has expanded wonderfully in every way! It's safe to give myself a chance.

~ DAY 337 ~

What GOOD could be possible?

In the middle of a restless night when my crazy thoughts and racing heart keep sleep at bay, I sit up in bed with a notebook and pen. At the top of the page I write "What GOOD could be possible?" Then I start writing whatever comes to mind. World peace, family relationships healed, financial security for all, self-forgiveness. After a while I sense the presence of my own inner wisdom, along with options yet unexplored. The light of possibility starts to shine by means of my own written word.

When I can't sleep, "What GOOD could be possible?"
allows my inner wisdom to speak to me through my own
written word.

~ DAY 338 ~

Holding the space for forgiveness

There's something genuinely inspiring about people who've been deeply hurt and have forgiven the perpetrator and also themselves. They often have the ability to hold the space for others who suffer from unforgiveness without trying to fix them. Somehow they realize that just by holding a space for forgiveness, they create an avenue for healing. They become a great gift to humanity.

I hold the space for forgiveness today—for others and for
myself.

~ Day 339 ~

There's more than enough

Our ancestors lived in a time of limited resources. They therefore competed with others to stay alive. They learned to be afraid. Our fear-based ego was born with the fight or flight mentality that kept us safe. This fear imprinted on our human brains. As we awaken to our spiritual essence we can lay aside our old fears with the spiritual truth of abundance—there's more than enough for everyone.

I lay my old fears to rest with the truth of abundance—there's more than enough for everyone.

~ Day 340 ~

New to planet Earth

Without even realizing it, our old negative expectations can get in the way of the joyous life we deserve. If you tend to worry, try this: Pretend you're new to planet Earth, saying hello for the first time. Greet each family member with a big smile! It changes your outlook and maybe their response! When your boss calls you into his or her office, anticipate good news! Give it a try and see what happens!

Pretending I'm new to planet Earth, I see with eyes of welcome and happy anticipation!

～ Day 341 ～

Feeling trapped

There have been times when my life felt trapped in a very small space—jobs or relationships that were no longer in my best interests. Because the process was gradual, I hadn't even realized I was feeling so confined. Then freedom beckoned, inviting me to break loose and live in a larger playing field, one that holds the next steps to my happiness and fulfillment. Gathering my courage, I broke loose and said yes!

Feeling trapped reminds me that it's time to break loose and live in a larger playing field.

～ Day 342 ～

Happiness in the simple things

I find joy in the simple things. I have pots of flowers on my condo patio. When I water them I try not to disturb the spider webs that show up in the springtime. Those little spiders are visitors in my garden, "Welcome to my home! Make a place among the beauty of the flowers. Let it become your home for as long as you like." Such simple things remind me when I notice, I feel my connection to all things, thus bringing happiness into my life.

Finding joy in the simple things brings happiness into my life.

~ DAY 343 ~

Breaking through resistance

I resisted going to Al-Anon for two years before I walked through the doors the first time. I didn't want to admit that I needed help, and I was afraid of the changes that would happen when I finally made the commitment. Yes, it was hard, and it was also vitally important. My life couldn't change until I changed. I bless the rooms of recovery—they gave me a brand new life and the God of my understanding.

Breaking through resistance, I become willing to change.

~ DAY 344 ~

Our earth is a gift

The Infinite One is such an incredible artist. Who else could think up the colors of the seasons? How else could the night sky become a canvas for brilliant sunsets, constellations, shooting stars and the aurora borealis? Who else could decorate the glory of creation that we see in our forests, prairies, meadows and oceans? Our earth is a gift from the One that adores us.

The earth is a gift from the One that adores me.

~ Day 345 ~

Permission to make a change

There are days when my life is a mess! On the outside it looks as if nothing's changed, but on the inside there's a growing disconnect. It's a reminder that my life can be so much more than I'm allowing it to be. Is it time to say no to something I'm doing and/or say yes to something brand new? My inner wisdom holds the answer—I give myself permission to make a change.

When it's time to make a change, I give myself permission to do so.

~ Day 346 ~

Morning coffee

When I pour my morning coffee, I sometimes think about all the others who are pouring their morning coffee—those who are celebrating and those in despair, those in happy relationships and those who are lonely, those who're afraid and those walking through their fear. Then I realize I'm all of them. In my heart there is no them and me—we're all one.

There is no them and me—we're all one.

~ Day 347 ~

Judgment creates a lonely place

When I judge another's lifestyle, I create a border. When I'm a critical of a friend's perspective or behavior, a wall goes up. When I find fault with the way a person looks, the wall gets higher. Soon I've boxed myself into a very lonely place where the only one who is right is me. No more! I break down the walls, cast aside the borders, lighten up, let go and join the world!

I gratefully let go of judgment to lighten up and join the world.

~ Day 348 ~

Surviving my problems

It's normal and natural for our human lives to include surviving our most difficult challenges—it's how we discover the stuff from which we're made. We get a glimpse of our strength, tenacity and courage every time we pick ourselves up to move through the challenge instead of becoming mired in it. In surviving our problems we live to transcend them.

Every time I survive a problem I discover a new level of my strength, tenacity and courage.

~ Day 349 ~

One choice at a time

I create the life of my dreams one choice at a time. If I say no to an activity I really don't want to do, I'm saying yes to all the things I do want to do. When I check out someplace brand new just for the fun of it, I'm expanding my willingness to discover new activities and adventures that may hold the key to more fun in my life. If I enjoy drawing a picture or writing a poem, I say yes to the belief that I'm creative and have something to say. My life moves forward one choice at a time.

Every time I say yes to a new choice that's for me, I say yes to a life that's for me.

~ Day 350 ~

Etch A Sketch

We tend to accumulate emotional baggage—the opinions of others plus our own judgments and hurt feelings. This accumulated baggage gets heavy! Remember Etch A Sketches? What if we lightened our load by pretending that our mind is an Etch A Sketch? We can gently shake our head, clearing our inner slate from that old baggage, making a space for a new beginning!

Pretending my mind is an Etch A Sketch, I clear my inner slate of emotional baggage.

~ Day 351 ~

Heart-to-heart

It's important to cultivate relationships that nourish us, surrounding ourselves with people who positively support us as we follow the path to manifesting our dreams. At the same time, we can notice if we're being supportive as the other person follows their dreams. Is it time for a heart-to-heart talk? Perhaps we can both make adjustments which will benefit the relationship!

As our relationships evolve, a heart-to-heart talk may benefit each person.

~ Day 352 ~

Learning from temptations

Life is filled with all kinds of temptations—that itch to say something I'll regret, eat the food that's not good for me, or settle for less than I'm worth. The enticement of temptations reminds me that I'm human—sometimes I do well and sometimes not so much. Temptations are opportunities to have the discipline to say no and also to offer myself compassion when I cave into them, learning from each experience.

No matter how I handle each temptation, I learn from the experience.

~ Day 353 ~

This works for me

Once I started on a spiritual path, I moved through life differently. It caught people's attention! Some asked me about the changes I'd made. Following my soul's guidance, I told them about it and added, "This works for me. You'll discover what works for you." Offering guidance without the need to control what their path should look like helped me realize how far I'd come.

My spiritual path works for me. Others will discover what works for them.

~ Day 354 ~

Uncovering my dreams

Listening to someone else talk about their dreams can open us up to parts of ourselves we may not have even been aware of. Their hopes and dreams may ignite a spark that loosens our own imaginings from their moorings, uncovering dreams that have been tucked away until now. Within the safety of our own heart, we are free to let our imagination soar to explore the far reaches of our desires.

I pay attention to my own heart's desires as I listen to another's dream.

~ Day 355 ~

I celebrate my kindness

You matter in the world. You were created from divine kindness. Offering kindness to yourself and others is normal and natural. Walking gently through the world is your nature. Today, try making a list of at least ten ways that you are kind to yourself and ten ways you're kind to others. If being kind to yourself is a stretch, your work begins there. Celebrate your kindness! You're worth it.

I pay attention to and celebrate the ways I'm kind to others and to myself.

~ Day 356 ~

My wounds can strengthen me

We all have wounds—they're part of the human experience. For some, evidence of our wounds can be seen. With others they're felt on the inside. Our wounds can cripple us, keeping us from trying to reach our goals, or they can grow our strength and resilience as we become the hero of our own story. Our dreams may have detoured, taking a new direction, but they aren't over.

My wounds strengthen me as I become the hero of my own story.

~ DAY 357 ~

Forgiveness in the moment

It's possible to consciously begin the process of forgiveness before the circumstance starts to fester. Our soul, the part of us that has never judged, is accessible in that moment. Leaning into its wisdom and grace, we can choose forgiveness the instant our heart tells us to pay attention. Forgiveness in the moment removes the need for resentment later on.

Accessing the wisdom of my soul, I begin the process of forgiveness the moment it's needed.

~ DAY 358 ~

Emotional maturity

Friendships take time, effort and emotional maturity. Even when we know our friends love and care about us, there will be times when we won't get our way and happiness is elusive. Friendships offer a chance to broaden our ability for understanding, peace and reconciliation, when appropriate putting another's needs before our own, which in turn assures our own feeling of generosity and well-being.

My friendships offer a space to grow understanding, peace and reconciliation.

~ Day 359 ~

My inner sanctuary

When I can no longer bear the weight that's so heavy on my shoulders, there's a sanctuary deep inside me where I can go. There I unburden my sorrows, laying down my grief to rest a while. I feel the embrace of the One that adores me, holding me in its grace. When I emerge, the world somehow looks and feels different—it holds new promise. In the quiet of this moment I can begin again.

> *Within my inner sanctuary I lay down my grief to rest a while. Emerging, I begin again.*

~ Day 360 ~

Down time

As I look back at my life, I notice instances when I got sick in order to allow myself to rest. I wasn't doing it consciously, but I was doing it nonetheless. I had such a strong work ethic that I didn't know how to balance it with rest as rejuvenation. Instead I thought rest was a waste of time and therefore wrong. Awareness is such a gift! Now I offer myself down time because I deserve a life that's balanced, rested and filled with joy.

> *Inviting balance into my life, I enjoy down time on a regular basis. I'm worth it!*

∼ DAY 361 ∼

My peace begins with me

I can create a life of peace, even when discord shows up. Turning away from drama—physically, mentally, and emotionally— is a choice. When others are upset with me for not joining the drama, it's my choice to say, "Sorry, this doesn't belong to me." Not buying into drama not only sets me free, it also creates a space for serenity, creativity and joy to flourish. The universe pays attention to my choices. It really does begin with me.

Turning away from drama, I create a space for peace to flourish in my life.

∼ DAY 362 ∼

Role models

I can change my attitude. I can change the way I talk about people and life events. I can change the way I think about myself. If I don't know how to do it, I can hang out with people who are good role models for me. I can watch how they do it. I can quit hanging out with people who see life negatively—I already know that doesn't work. I can learn from those who have a new perspective.

I hang out with people who are good role models for me, learning to see with a new perspective.

~ Day 363 ~

Underwear counts!

What's one little thing you can do to take care of yourself today? Light a candle as you get ready for your day, read something uplifting, look in the mirror and tell yourself, "You're awesome!" wear clothes you really like (underwear counts!), sing a song to your pet, eat something different and yummy for breakfast. Congratulate yourself for noticing what makes you happy and then doing it! Maybe you can do it again tomorrow!

> *Today I will do at least one thing just for me because it makes me happy!*

~ Day 364 ~

Gaining confidence

As my world expands, the roads I used to travel fade away, inviting me to take new paths. If left to my own devices, the fear of the unknown would paralyze me. Instead I lean into the wisdom of my soul, allowing it to lead me. With each step forward I gain confidence as freedom's pull becomes stronger than the fear that's trying to stop me.

> *Freedom's pull is stronger than the fear that's trying to stop me.*

~ Day 365 ~

With gratitude

Dear Beloved One,

Thank you for those times when I could hardly catch my breath from crying so hard and for the lonely nights when I doubted myself. Thank you for every single problem that challenged me to be the person I want to be. Sometimes I moved through it well and sometimes I made a mess of it, but still I kept going. I like who I am today. Thank you for believing in me.

When I doubt myself, the One who believes in me helps me keep going.

Index

Faith

Fear

Forgiveness

Freedom

Friendships

ABOUT
JANE BEACH

For the first fifty years of her life Jane Beach was an atheist. In a moment of awareness, she discovered that the God of her understanding was real. Her whole life changed and much to her surprise, she became a minister! Jane's passion is her love affair with the one she calls the Beloved. Jane's writings invite readers to investigate their own love affair with the divine ... their own inner beauty. Her personal relationship with life is contagious, and wherever she shows up an atmosphere of possibility, acceptance and unconditional love abound.

Jane is now happily retired and has become a budding artist. She lives in Santa Rosa, California, writing, painting, and walking among the trees and wild turkeys.

You can email Jane at **revjanebeach@janebeach.com**, connect with her on Facebook at **www.facebook.com/RevJaneBeach** and find her paintings on Etsy at **www.etsy.com/shop/JaneBeachART**

ABOUT THE PUBLISHER

Kenos Press™, an imprint of Six Degrees Publishing Group™, publishes literary works which are meant to encourage an intimate connection with the Divine, uplift the human spirit, and further peace by improving our universal connection with one another.

Learn more about Kenos Press at our link on the web at:
SixDegreesPublishing.com

CPSIA information can be obtained
at www.ICGtesting.com
Printed in the USA
LVHW102038200323
742068LV00029B/957